THE
SACRAMENT
OF
Happy

The general definition of sacrament is "a visible sign of inward grace," which in communities of faith most often refers to holy communion or the Eucharist. However, in the broadest understanding a sacrament is a gift bestowed by God and in that case "happiness" is absolutely a sacrament—a visible, sometimes even audible, sign of inward grace!

THE
SACRAMENT
OF
Happy

What a Smiling God
Brings to a Wounded World

LISA HARPER

B&H
PUBLISHING GROUP
NASHVILLE, TENNESSEE

Published by B&H Publishing Group
Nashville, Tennessee

Dewey Decimal Classification: 158
Subject Heading: HAPPINESS \ JOY AND SORROW \ CHRISTIAN
LIFE

Cover and biography photographs by Mandy Johnson.

4 5 6 7 8 9 10 • 22 21 20 19 18

To my daughter, Melissa Price Harper, who—other than my salvation—is the greatest gift God has lavished me with and whose happy giggle makes my whole world go 'round.

Acknowledgments

LATE BISHOP LESSLIE NEWBIGIN ASSERTED COMMUNITY was one of the most effective hermeneutics of the gospel—in other words, that we see Jesus more clearly through the lens of the other Christ-followers we get to rub shoulders with. And that has certainly been my experience. I'm indebted to an incredible community of family, friends, and colleagues who helped breathe life into this project.

Chief among them is my very dear friend Christine Caine, who would surely drag me toward Jesus if I got discouraged and attempted to tap out on this journey of faith!

I'm also beyond grateful for Lisa Jackson, my literary agent/ coach/confidant, who champions me with way more grace than I deserve.

I can't overstate how awesome and riddled with integrity and creativity the entire publishing team at LifeWay is, but I must give special kudos to Heather Nunn, my dedicated-far-beyond-the-call-of-duty editor, and Jennifer Lyell, the head honcho of B&H and the godliest gambler I know because she definitely took a chance on me!

I'm also deeply grateful for the constancy of two Bible study "sisterhoods" that I get to do life with on Tuesdays at Belle's house and Wednesdays at my home church, Grace Chapel.

And last but certainly not least, I'm truly blessed to have a loving, patient, and supportive family who never complains about my penchant for mining the colorful hills of our genealogy for storytelling jewels!

Contents

Foreword

I LOVE LISA HARPER. SHE IS A GIFT TO THE BODY OF Christ and to me. Over the years, we have laughed together—and cried together—a lot. She is one of my closest confidants—someone I know I can talk to openly and trust with the depths of my heart. I love how she always directs me to God's Word, His love, and His grace, and being around her simply makes me a happier person.

I first met Lisa when we were both scheduled to speak at a women's conference. I cried and laughed throughout her message and knew we were destined to be forever friends. As I got to know her and grew to love her, her life story unfolded. She was a brilliant Bible teacher and great lover of people who served faithfully in ministry all her adult life—but there was one goal she had yet to achieve. She wanted to be a mom, and repeated adoption opportunities had fallen through. Despite her heartache, I was always aware that Lisa was still happy and in love with Jesus! She was happy even though her life was less than perfect and her deep yearning for a child was unfulfilled. That's because her happiness was rooted in something far deeper than circumstances going her way. She had learned a deep truth that anchored her life and ministry.

That powerful truth is what she uncovers in *The Sacrament of Happy*.

The Sacrament of Happy is one more reflection of her deeply intimate relationship with God—and her powerful insight into His character. Page after page, she walks us into deeper understanding and acceptance of His passionate desire for all of us to live happy. I'm so thankful God has spoken this message through her to us because it's not something we all know how to walk in. In fact, many of us wonder if it is even biblical for Christians to be happy. It is no accident that you are holding this book in your hand; you are about to discover one of the greatest keys to true freedom you could ever have.

Learning to live happy has been a critical part of my own journey to freedom because I didn't grow up around very happy people. I grew up the daughter of Greek immigrants—in a culture of fatalists. My Greek family and extended community believed that no matter how bad things are, they can always grow worse. Speaking out of this mentality, my mother always thought FIRST of the worst possible scenario that could happen . . .

"Christina, are you wearing clean underwear? You don't want to be in an accident and not have clean underwear on." (Despite the fact I actually did have a skiing accident once and had to go to the hospital not wearing any underwear under my base layer is beside the point. If I'd had any on, surely they would have been clean.)

My mother truly believed . . .

- *You can't have your cake—and eat it too.*
- *If it's too good to be true—then it is.*
- *If it can go wrong—it will.*
- *Everything that goes up—must come down.*
- *Keep both feet on the ground—and your head out of the clouds.*
- *Don't count your chickens—until they hatch.*

Her motto was to live safe and risk-free—and you may experience happiness occasionally, but don't expect to very often. After all, life is hard, suffering is everywhere, and hopes and dreams are shattered. "Christine, expect disappointment and you will never be disappointed." Why she was unhappy was understandable—but staying unhappy wasn't. Long before I was born, she and my father fled Egypt following the Egyptian Revolution of 1952. Their traumatic escape after the coup to find safety in Australia led to living with a sense of fear and anxiety, a sense of sadness and loss—and it never left them. Like so many of the families I grew up with in our Greek community and church, they never knew happiness—and they wore their sadness like a badge of honor.

Today, as I travel and speak, I meet people who live the same way. They haven't overcome a tragic childhood or some terrible experience they endured . . .

- Losing a child
- Closing their company
- Watching their marriage unravel
- Foreclosing on a home
- Spiraling out of control with addiction
- Unrealized dreams

So they live hopeless, depressed, bitter, hard, isolated. They battle with being fearful of the future, confident that it won't be good. They've lost their joy—and don't know how to find it.

That journey back to happiness is what Lisa so beautifully illustrates in this book. She directs our attention to Jesus—over and over again. She directs our attention to the truth He spoke: "The thief does not come except to steal, and to kill, and to destroy. I have come that they may have life, and that they may have it more abundantly" (John 10:10 NKJV).

Lisa makes it clear: God wants us to be happy! And it's not something we have to wait until heaven to enjoy. Right here, in the midst of pain, God wants us to experience a taste of heaven on earth every day. He encourages us to live joyful: "Rejoice in the Lord always, and again, I say, rejoice" (Phil. 4:4).

In her brilliant yet personable style, Lisa shows us how happiness is not something that happens externally—like finding a new romance, buying a new car, or getting a big promotion.

It's something that happens internally. It's developing a perspective of looking higher. An attitude of believing for the best. A transformation of the heart that trusts Jesus no matter what. A life that looks forward to the future.

The message of *The Sacrament of Happy* is very personal to me. Building on the same principles Lisa outlines in this book, Nick and I have built a home where happiness is highly valued. We want our girls to live happy far more often than they are sad or mad—the same way God intends for us to live.

We've built our ministry on these principles as well. Being involved in rescuing the victims of human trafficking gives us a front-row seat to seeing the worst of humanity in the traffickers—and the powerful beauty of God's restoration in those we rescue. The only way for our team not to be overwhelmed by the darkness is to ensure they are happy at the core of their being by staying connected to Jesus. By abiding in the vine, by staying connected, they can bear much fruit (John 15:1–17).

The Sacrament of Happy—like all of Lisa's messages and books—enriches my understanding of God and His Word—and his great love for us. As always, she unfolds biblical truth so clearly and calls me to action. Every. Single. Time.

—Christine Caine
Founder, A21 & Propel Women

CHAPTER
ONE

Is Happy Even Holy?

___

Every man, whatsoever his condition,
desires to be happy.[1]
St. Augustine

A FEW YEARS AGO ONE OF MY DEAR FRIENDS, SHEILA
Walsh, and I were invited to walk the red carpet for the premiere
of another friend's movie. But don't picture a typical red carpet
premiere seen on television or in magazines! Imagine more of a
burgundy indoor/outdoor polypropylene floor covering kind of
event taking place at a multiplex in the suburbs next to several
fast-food restaurants. Suffice it to say, we were tickled before we
even got there.

1

Sheila's husband, Barry, chauffeured us to the event since we weren't sure we could walk—much less drive—in our snug, fancy dresses. We parked at the edge of the lot so we'd have privacy to make any necessary hair and makeup adjustments before facing the swelling crowd of eight or nine people who'd gathered to meet us. While the place he parked was private, it was—unbeknownst to us—also next to a grassy median that was soggy from recent rain. Therefore, when Sheila lifted her gold silk skirt and stepped gracefully out of the car onto the adjacent turf, her four-inch heels were immediately sucked into the mud, rendering her flailing and stuck like a stork in quicksand.

I sprang into action, heroically yelling for her to hang on while I attempted to squeeze myself out of the back seat of Barry's claustrophobic, two-door sports car that was obviously designed by sadists. Two broken fingernails and one snagged sleeve later, I finally emerged to render her aid, but as soon as I grabbed Sheila's arm to pull her to dry land, the heels of my shoes pierced through the muck, effectively pinning me in place too. We grabbed each other frantically like two sailors who realize their ship is going down fast and they've missed the opportunity to jump overboard. As we toppled over in an ungainly heap, I really had no option but to fall squarely on top of my more petite pal. After much futile slipping and sliding, we began laughing hysterically and momentarily lost the ability to stand—even had we been able to find some leverage. At which point from somewhere underneath me, Sheila squeaked, "Help me. I'm peeing and I can't stop."

Sheila and I were together at a conference recently and got to regale some new friends at dinner afterward with the silly story of our "peetastrophe"—which lit the fuse for others to tell their most embarrassing stories. After much communal hilarity, the woman sitting next to me leaned back into her chair and said with a sigh, "Wow, those were happy times, weren't they?" As everyone around the table smiled and nostalgically agreed, I found myself thinking, *Why do we tend to speak of happy in the past or future tense—like, "Those were happy times," or "Won't we be happy when . . ."—as if happy were some fleeting, ephemeral state that we can only reminisce about or pine for?* I then found myself pondering the concept of happiness further: "Since the Bible says every good gift is from God and happy is good, I wonder if happy is actually a gift from God—a sacrament of sorts? And if that's the case, we could actually be happy *now* and stay happy *then*. Hmmm."

It's a wonderful concept, isn't it? But can we prove its validity?

One highly qualified educator and PhD, Dr. Emma Seppälä, the science director of Stanford University's Center for Compassion and Altruism Research and Education, defines happiness as: *a state of heightened positive emotion* and trumpets its potential: "Happiness has a profound positive effect on our professional and personal lives. It increases our emotional and social intelligence, boosts our productivity, and heightens our influence over peers and colleagues. These are the very ingredients that allow us to be successful without having to sacrifice our health and psychological well-being."² A pretty good start to understanding happiness, don't you think?

As secular as it may sound at first, "seeking happiness" does not have to be a hedonistic, self-indulgent pursuit. In fact, ancient church father and puritan Thomas Manton asserted that our desire for happiness is completely natural: "It is natural for the reasonable creature to desire to be happy, as it is for the fire to burn."³ And modern-day minister and author Randy Alcorn went a step further in his recent book, *Happiness*, by not only proving God wired us to seek happiness but said that censoring that divine urge is dangerous: "The modern evangelical antipathy to happiness backfires when it portrays Christianity as being against what people long for most."⁴

I used to think happiness and holiness were divergent paths. It took a panic attack to shock me into the pursuit of genuine, God-authored happiness. Interestingly enough, it was while I was teaching a Bible study. When I was about halfway through the message—on authenticity of all things—my heart began to beat wildly and I began to sweat profusely. This wasn't a glowing sheen like athletic models wear either. I mean, rivulets were running down my face, soaking my shirt and the seat of my pants! I kept speaking and acted casually, as if it were totally normal for my body to produce copious amounts of perspiration, but inwardly I thought, *Uh-oh, I think* Readers Digest *listed this as the sign of an impending heart attack. But I'm pretty sure it said you'd also have a tingling sensation in your right arm if it were a heart attack. Or maybe it was the left arm? Oh crud, I really don't want to have a heart attack right here right now.*

After I rambled and spurted for several more absurdly long minutes, the sweat began to trickle down the backs of my legs all the way to my calves. I felt completely disassociated with my body as if I were floating a few feet away from it. I watched—in what seemed like a drunken state—a woman in the crowd frown, lean over to her friend, and whisper, "Is she okay?" Then in blurry slow motion, I stammered a benediction and stumbled off the stage.

Thirty minutes or so later (after the projectile perspiration subsided, my heartbeat slowed down to normal, and I convinced a few concerned friends that I wasn't having a heart attack), I got into my car, called a therapist, and made the first appointment of what turned into almost a decade of digging. When you've become a master faker like I had, the truth gets buried pretty deep. While I believe that all of life's answers can be found in God's Word, I've realized I often need the help of those wiser than me to find them and apply them to the most wounded places of my heart. Sometimes we need triage before we can get back up and fight the good fight. Before we can actually participate in the fullness of joy instead of just pretending we're happy.

Although I never heard "God will be disappointed in you if you don't pull yourself up by your bootstraps" in a sermon as a child—at least not verbatim—I'd observed it consistently demonstrated by adult churchgoers. By the time I was in the first grade, the scaffolding of my budding theology included a firm belief in self-sufficiency and optimism. I sincerely thought that sad = bad. So I learned how to wear a happy expression and speak with a happy inflection, even when sadness lurked beneath my emotional surface like a great white shark in a cold, dark sea.

And emotional sharks aren't content slinking around below the surface forever. Every now and then, they bite. By the time I was in high school, I'd developed migraine headaches that had gotten so intense they were causing me to have blackouts and get violently sick every couple of weeks. After I lost consciousness at track practice one afternoon, Mom raced me to a neurologist who immediately admitted me to a hospital because I had multiple symptoms of a brain tumor.

A battery of tests—including a full psych consult—concluded there was a build-up of cerebrospinal fluid behind my optic nerve, not a brain tumor or anything else life-threatening. Other than dealing with the extreme awkwardness of several relatives sobbing uncontrollably in my hospital room after hovering outside the doorway and talking with Mom in hushed tones (the women in our family aren't always adept at dealing with sad, but we are quite gifted at drama), that four-day hospital stay wasn't as grim as my family initially feared.

However, it didn't seem to be very beneficial either because after explaining my condition to Mom, the neurologist declared ominously that besides a potentially fatal operation that involved installing a shunt in my head, which *might* help drain the excess fluid, or by putting me on powerful, anti-seizure meds, there was no other viable treatment. He added dismissively that there was a chance it would resolve itself after the hormonal fluctuations of puberty leveled out. Then he ended the consultation by sternly cautioning me against competitive athletics, being outside in the sun, and eating cheese or nuts. (Of course, even then I knew that being a pale, lethargic couch potato bereft of chips and queso was far worse than a little fainting and vomiting every now and then, so I was not a submissive patient. Fortunately, by my freshman year in college, the keeling and retching had become only a rare occurrence.)

I'd all but forgotten about that hospital stay until I was in my early forties and my counselor and I were excavating some of the bigger hills of my adolescence. I remembered an alarming, thoroughly-dismissed-at-the-time, symptom from that long-ago health scare and recalled it vividly because I'd heard Mom tell this story numerous times when I was in my teens and twenties. During the psych consult, a child psychiatrist met with me—part of their normal protocol at the time when treating a minor—to ascertain whether he thought there were any signs of child abuse or mental illness. Following our two-hour visit, he sat down with Mom to go over his evaluation. Once he'd explained that he found no signs of physical abuse or psychosis, he closed my file, took off his glasses, rubbed the bridge of his nose, and said soberly, "Mrs. Angel, Lisa is either the most happy, well-adjusted child I've ever met in my life, or she is in deep emotional pain."

Every time my dear mama got to the end of that story at a family gathering or while discussing me *in front of me* with a grocery store clerk or a saleslady behind the makeup counter in the mall, her voice would rise triumphantly because she regarded the psychiatrist's statement as proof that I *was* the happiest, most well-adjusted child in the history of the universe.

It took me two and a half decades to realize that compassionate doctor was trying to tell my mom I was a pretty little liar—my mirth was mostly a mirage. Unfortunately, by the time I was a teenager we'd been pretending for so long that I suppose we all felt safer to continue dogpaddling on the surface, rather than diving deep enough to deal with the sharks. And while young adulthood brought with it the growing awareness that the painful knots in my soul stemmed from childhood wounds—my parents' very acrimonious divorce and the sexual molestation I experienced as a little girl by several different men—I had no idea how to deal with them. So, when I graduated from college, took a job in youth ministry, and became a "professional" Christian, I felt like I had no choice but to suppress any "bad" feelings and smile. Eventually, I became a master happy doppelgänger.

Will the Real Happy Please Stand Up

Webster defines *happy* a little differently than—although not contradictory to—Dr. Seppälä:

> happy [hap-ee]: *characterized by or indicative of pleasure, contentment, or joy*[5]

Happy. The word itself conjures up idyllic images, doesn't it? Like a toddler in overalls splashing through puddles while gleefully chasing a frog. Or a couple of kindergartners sitting elbow to elbow at a picnic table both wearing gap-toothed grins and holding slices of watermelon bigger than their heads. Or a bright-eyed cheerleader who's catapulted high in the air with her arms over her head in victory when the home team scores the winning touchdown. Or a bespectacled young man with too much hair gel and a sparsely-bearded chin beaming at his prom date with the smitten glow of young love. *Happy.* The kind of word a middle school girl might doodle in her diary with big loopy *p*'s and a flower woven into the tail of the *y*, right? *Happy.* It sounds like fireworks, smells like roasted marshmallows, and feels like cannon-balling into a cold pool on a hot day, doesn't it? What it does *not* seem to be is theologically sound. Surely *happy* is too circumstantially based, too emotive, too . . . well, too *unspiritual* to be an appropriate consistent state for Christ-followers, right?

Wrong. Wildly, sadly, distorted-by-religious-Pharisees-for-far-too-long WRONG.

There are actually thirty-seven references to "happy" in the
Old Testament and forty-eight in the New Testament. Randy
Alcorn's book, *Happiness,* became an encyclopedia for me while
researching my book. In it, he notes more than 2,700 passages
where terms related to happy—*gladness, merriment, pleasure, celebration, cheer, laughter, delight, jubilation,* and *feasting*—are used![6]
In fact, Psalms—the book smack-dab in the middle of the Bible
and comprised of 150 Old Testament *songs*[7]—literally begins with
the word *happy*:

> How *happy* is the one who does not walk in the advice
> of the wicked or stand in the pathway with sinners or sit
> in the company of mockers! Instead, his delight is in the
> LORD's instruction, and he meditates on it day and night.
> He is like a tree planted by flowing streams that bears its
> fruit in its season and whose leaf does not wither. Whatever
> he does prospers. (Ps. 1:1–3, emphasis mine)

And the Sermon on the Mount—arguably Jesus' most beloved
message—could accurately be titled, "How to Be Happy" since it
technically begins with the word *happy* as well:

> "Happy the poor in spirit—because theirs is the reign of
> the heavens.
>
> Happy the mourning—because they shall be
> comforted.
>
> Happy the meek—because they shall inherit the land.

Happy those hungering and thirsting for righteousness—because they shall be filled.

Happy the kind—because they shall find kindness.

Happy the clean in heart—because they shall see God.

Happy the peacemakers—because they shall be called Sons of God.

Happy those persecuted for righteousness' sake—because theirs is the reign of the heavens.

Happy are ye whenever they may reproach you, and may persecute, and may say any evil thing against you falsely for my sake—

rejoice ye and be glad, because your reward [is] great in the heavens, for thus did they persecute the prophets who were before you." (Matt. 5:3–12 YLT)

Therefore, while with most translations we hear this read from the beginning with the term *blessed*—which admittedly has a more old-school, shiny wooden pew ring to it—beginning Psalm 1 with the term *happy* is every bit as theologically sound. Because the English transliteration of the Hebrew word in the original text of Psalm 1 is *asre*[8] or Asher which can be translated *either* "happy" or "blessed."[9] In the same vein, the Beatitudes typically begin with the English word *blessed*, but the original Greek word *blessed* is translated from is *makarios*, which can also be translated "happy" or "fortunate."[10]

That means *happy* is not only a holy sacrament, it's a covenant state of being for God's people.

Wow. That has the potential to flat-out blow your theological hard-drive, doesn't it? Especially if, like me, you've digested a lot of well-intentioned sermons emphasizing the value of *joy* (often taught to be based on what Jesus accomplished for us on the cross and/or the philosophy **J**esus-**O**thers-**Y**ourself) versus *happy* (often taught to be based on our circumstances; what happens *to us*). When I first began wrestling with the idea that *happy* and *joy* are more like fraternal twins than distant cousins, I felt like I was being naughty—like running with biblical scissors or playing with scriptural matches. I mean, *holy* or *faithful* are mainstays of church vernacular and perennial worship lyric favorites, so they're obviously on the approved behavior list for believers. And *pious* actually sounds spiritual . . . like some advanced state of Christlikeness only possible with lots of straining and grimacing, akin to a master yoga pose (but without all the Eastern mysticism or questionable workout attire, of course). But the fact that *happy* made God's list of laudable behavior sounds almost too good to be true.

Thankfully, it's not. Contrary to what many of us have been taught or perceived, Christ-followers aren't called to jettison our happiness like spiritual floaties as we learn to swim in the deep waters of intimacy with God. Instead, we're quite literally *called* to be happy.

Too Good Not to Be God's Truth

My most recent tour guide to "too good to not be God's truth" happy-town was a toilet. Okay, maybe that sounds a bit anthropomorphic: obviously, toilets can't talk, much less in the perky tone a tour guide job requires. So I'll rephrase and say a porcelain throne was the proverbial bucket I used to dip in the well from which my happy flows. Actually, to be more accurate, an *overflowing* commode was the well from which my happy flowed. These metaphors are going downhill fast, aren't they? Perhaps it would help if I back up (puns are really hard to avoid when a potty is at the center of the story) and start from the beginning.

Indoor plumbing was a luxury in the Haitian village where my adopted daughter, Missy, grew up. And soft, two-ply toilet paper? That was even more rare. Therefore, when I finally brought her home to Tennessee, toilet-flushing in our house with copious amounts of Charmin quickly became one of her favorite pastimes. *Darling*, was my thought early on as I observed the wide-eyed delight she displayed while watching massive plumes of paper spiral downward. I wasn't even bothered when I had to call the plumber the first few times. But after a while, wading through ankle-deep wastewater in my bathroom (for some reason, she's partial to mine and has never once flooded the facilities in hers) and writing large checks to repairmen lost its allure.

I gave her cheerful lectures regarding the benefits of judicious toilet paper consumption. After that ceased to dissuade her from sending an entire forest down the drain during one particularly energetic, unsupervised potty episode, I grew more creative in my water-the-floor-no-more campaign and made up this catchy tune: "Five squares is where it's at, only moms need more'n 'dat. Tissue wads are so not cool, use single strips on the stool!" When this winsome strategy failed, and my bathroom floor showed signs of warping, I employed more punitive consequences for her messy infractions; I limited iPad usage and confiscated one of her favorite Paw Patrol figurines. But nothing seemed to stem the tide.

To put it mildly, I was at my wit's end when I walked into my bathroom a few months ago—past my innocent-looking daughter taking a bubble bath (she also likes my bathtub more than hers because it's bigger and "splashier")—slipped on wet tile, and quickly discovered water gushing out of the commode like Niagara Falls. After a heavy sigh, I morphed into the put-on persona my mother used when I did something especially naughty as a child:

Doggone it, Melissa, HOW MANY TIMES DO I HAVE TO TELL YOU that You. Do. Not. Use. Giant. Gobs. Of. Toilet. Paper. Like. This? And good night, if you ARE going to use an entire roll of toilet paper in one sitting, the least you could do is flush several times so I don't have to deal with a disgusting mess like this! Dadgummit, I am So. Tired. Of. This, Missy! Why didn't you tell me you'd stopped up the toilet again and water was all over the floor?

The entire time I was plunging and fussing and mopping up that yucky pond with beach towels, I had my back to Missy.

Within a minute or two—after my irritability had subsided enough to realize she hadn't responded to my question—I turned around and was immediately convicted by the sight of my precious little girl sitting ramrod straight and staring at me mournfully as big tears streamed down her beautiful brown cheeks. I had all but crushed her spirit over something innocent and insignificant. She wasn't *trying* to cause a mess. She hadn't been willfully disobedient or disrespectful, so it wasn't a heart or character issue. It was a plumbing issue.

I lifted her out of the tub, dried her off with our last dry towel, and rocked her back and forth until she stopped crying. I carefully explained that it was wrong for Mama to raise her voice, that I'd made a very bad choice, and that I was so sorry I'd hurt her feelings. Once she fell asleep, I called my contractor. When he answered the phone, his voice belied the fact that he was a little perplexed at my nighttime summons. He was thrown even further off balance when after a quick hello I asked the following question: "Hey, Jack, you know those really powerful toilets they have on cruise ships that feel like they could suck your leg off when you flush them? Are they available for residential use?" After I explained *why* I wanted to replace our regular old Home Depot type of commode with a supersonic vacuum version, he chuckled and said he'd get one the next day and install it right away. Less than forty-eight hours later, our brand-new appliance was installed, and I cheered so enthusiastically after Missy's inaugural flush, you'd have thought she'd won an Olympic medal!

Our recent toiletastrophe effectively reminded me of how much I love, value, and cherish my little girl. Even more importantly, it reminded me of how much God the Father loves, values, and cherishes me, His kid. I continue to be overwhelmed at the beautiful, juxtaposed, redemptive ways of God in my life—how He chose a former Haitian orphan, who lost her first mom to AIDS and never knew her biological father, to rip out the last stubborn roots of the orphaned, fatherless spirit that's been growing in my heart since before I was her age. God continues to employ my unlikely, only-by-grace, position of motherhood as a constant, colorful illustration of how He cheers Himself hoarse over every ungainly cartwheel His children do in His glorious backyard. How He makes over every stick-figure drawing we present to Him in our mostly narcissistic prayers and displays it on His refrigerator in glory. How despite our proclivity to make huge messes, He is so completely for us. How *He is good, He does good,* and oh how He wants us to be happy!

May all those who seek you be happy and rejoice in you! (Ps. 40:16 NET)

The Practical Pursuit of Happiness

1. Do you tend to imagine God the Father with a smiling countenance or more of a somber expression?

   _____

   _____

   _____

2. What about Jesus the Son—is it more natural for you to picture Him laughing or brooding?

   _____

   _____

   _____

3. What kind of emotional sharks have lurked beneath the surface of your "false-positive" exterior in the past?

   _____

   _____

   _____

4. When, where, and with whom are you most likely to suppress your sad or "bad" feelings?

   _____

   _____

   _____

5. How would you concisely define *happiness*?

    _____

    _____

    _____

6. Do you think the people who know you best would describe
    you as happy? Why or why not?

    _____

    _____

    _____

7. What aspect of "happy" still seems a bit superficial, unspiri-
    tual, or even sacrilegious to you (if any)?

    _____

    _____

    _____

CHAPTER TWO

Is God Happy?

*Where others see but the dawn coming over the
hill, I see the soul of God shouting for joy.*[1]
William Blake

MY DAD WAS A TOOTSIE-ROLL-POP KIND OF GUY—HARD ON
the outside but soft on the inside. Much like the dense, you-might-
break-your-teeth-if-you-try-to-bite-it-too-quickly exterior of those
suckers, Dad's veneer was thick and tough, so it took awhile to
get to the tender. And if you finally whittled your way there, it
was fleeting. Like a comet. Or one of those really incredible Black
Friday doorbuster deals.

One of my fondest memories of Dad's soft side happened when I was about ten—a few years after he and Mom divorced. He picked me up from school that Friday afternoon to spend the weekend with him, Lucy, and Ricky (my stepmom and stepbrother). Friday afternoons should've been the norm according to the visitation agreement, but I learned to keep my paternal expectations in check because Dad only showed up about half the time. Anyway, on this particular Friday when he *did* show, and after sharing our usual brief, sweetly strained reunion dialogue, we settled into the companionable silence that felt more comfortable to both of us—a silence broken periodically by the sound of him spitting tobacco juice into a white Styrofoam cup he kept in his truck.

I remember feeling happy when Dad turned the truck onto a familiar two-lane road that led to his friend's farm. Stopping at Mr. Robbie's had become a familiar routine. I knew he'd saunter out of the house in his highway patrol uniform, ruffle my hair, and then hand me an apple or carrot or several sugar cubes so I could go down to the barn. His pet horse, Gypsy, and I bonded while he and Dad talked about whatever it is monosyllabic men discuss. Gypsy was a two-year-old, half-wild American Quarter Horse with a reddish coat, jet-black mane, and ground-brushing tail, with one white sock on her front leg and a star on her forehead. She was the most beautiful creature I'd ever seen.

Initially she wouldn't let me get close to her. When I approached the fence, she would rear up on her hind legs, paw the air menacingly, whirl around in a ferocious spray of hoofs and dirt, and race to the farthest corner of the pasture. But then, Mr. Robbie would put his thumb and middle finger in his mouth and whistle a loud rebuke, and she'd come thundering back up toward us so fast that I'd think surely she was going to run right through the barbwire and trample me. To my amazement, she always skidded to a stop mere inches from the boundary wire, with flared nostrils and wide-eyes, tossing her massive head to and fro with derisive snorts that inevitably—and I'm sure *intentionally*—doused me with foamy spittle.

I was smitten. The first time she finally edged close enough to snatch an apple out of my open palm, my heart smiled. The first time she ran toward my whistle, my heart squealed. The first time she lowered her nose to nuzzle my shoulder, my heart melted. So when Dad walked up beside me that afternoon long ago and said, "She sure is something, isn't she?" I replied with reverent enthusiasm, "Yes, Sir!" He placed his hand firmly on my shoulder for a second or two, then gave me a hard pat and said gruffly, "Well, then come help me hitch up the trailer because I just bought her for you."

I sat on my haunches in the bed of the truck—as close as I could possibly get to the horse trailer—talking in soothing tones to my new high-strung companion and feeling like it was all a dream the whole way to Dad's farm. Somehow Daddy had peered into my heart, glimpsed my greatest wish, and made it come true. For a ten-year-old little girl whose favorite movie was *Black Beauty* and who doodled horses in all of her school

notebooks, Gypsy was a gift of epic proportions, an untamed trea-
sure of inestimable worth.

It took months for her to be saddle-trained and, more than
once, I was flung to the hard-packed Central Florida clay so hard it
knocked the wind out of me, but her undomesticated nature didn't
dim my joy. I mean, how can one resent the wind when it whips
through a forest, causing branches to crash to the ground? Instead,
you fling your arms wide open and exult in the sheer power of its
nature. And that's kind of what riding Gypsy was like . . . it was
like perching on the wind. She became my closest confidant; a safe
partner to pour out concerns about my new stepparents on long
solo rides, a big shoulder to press my face into and weep because
of the molestation no one knew about that made me feel so small
and dirty and powerless. I will probably always associate the smell
of hay with safety and security because of the special bond I had
with that horse.

But my dad didn't really believe in affectionate bonds between
animals and people. Instead, he believed it was necessary to exert
stern control over them—whether pets or livestock—lest they
become unmanageable or even dangerous. And the more Gypsy
resisted his attempts to domesticate her wild spirit, the harsher he
disciplined her. Once, while he was bent over cleaning debris out
of her front hoof, she lowered her head and playfully nipped his
straw cowboy hat. Only it didn't feel playful to Dad. Because his
hat was so thin, her giant teeth broke through and opened a small
divot on top of his head, which started to bleed. He jumped up in

a flash, smacked her hard between the eyes with the heavy metal farrier tool he'd been using on her hooves, and yelled an expletive with such furious indignation that I stumbled backwards away from him as my horse buckled and whinnied pitifully.

Experiencing both the unexpected kindness and the unforeseen rage of my father, often in close succession, taught me to create buffers between authority figures and myself. Especially men. Because, I reasoned, you never knew if they were going to hug you or hit you. Unfortunately, my early misconception about dads colored the lens through which I viewed my heavenly Father. From my earliest memory, I believed in God and respected His absolute authority, but I thought it best to keep a safe distance just in case He decided to smack me or someone I loved. I longed for His affection but was wary of scooting close enough for an embrace. I didn't necessarily picture Him as angry, but I certainly didn't imagine Him *happy*. Of course, I hoped God had a soft side and hoped to experience it one day, but I pictured Him more as an unsmiling kind of King. Which, based on an informal poll I took with a bunch of close friends recently, seems to be a common misconception. All of them are committed followers of Jesus Christ. Most of them used the word *holy* to describe God—which is true. But only one used the word *happy.*

What about you—have you ever ascribed the characteristic of "happy" to God? What about your friends? How about taking an informal poll of your close community of Christ-followers?

—

When I first started searching the Scriptures in an attempt to answer the question "Is God happy?" with theological surety, I was stunned by what I found and wondered how in the world I'd waded through these passages for decades and completely missed the gleaming gold lying just beneath the surface. For instance, in the English Standard Version Bible, 1 Timothy 1:11 reads like this:

> . . . in accordance with the *gospel* of the glory of the *blessed* God with which I have been entrusted. (emphasis mine)

The word *gospel* in the original Greek text is *euangelion*, which literally translated means "good news,"[2] and the word *blessed* is the most common scriptural translation of the Greek word *makarios*, which we've already established also means "happy" or "fortunate." Therefore, it would be just as accurate to translate 1 Timothy 1:11 like this:

> . . . in accordance with the good news of the glory of the happy God with which I have been entrusted.

In his marvelous classic, *The Pleasures of God*, pastor and theologian John Piper expounds on apostle Paul's use of "happy" in this pastoral letter: "It was inconceivable to the apostle Paul that God could be denied infinite joy and still be all-glorious. To be infinitely glorious was to be infinitely happy. He used the phrase, 'the glory of the happy God,' because it is a glorious thing for God to be as happy as he is. God's glory consists much in the fact that he is happy beyond our wildest imagination."[3]

The good news of the glory of the happy God takes on even more significance in the context of Jesus' parable of the talents in Matthew's gospel account:

"For it is just like a man about to go on a journey. He called his own servants and entrusted his possessions to them. To one he gave five talents, to another two talents, and to another one talent, depending on each one's ability. Then he went on a journey. Immediately the man who had received five talents went, put them to work, and earned five more. In the same way the man with two earned two more. But the man who had received one talent went off, dug a hole in the ground, and hid his master's money.

"After a long time the master of those servants came and settled accounts with them. The man who had received five talents approached, presented five more talents, and said, 'Master, you gave me five talents. See, I've earned five more talents.'

"His master said to him, 'Well done, good and faithful servant! You were faithful over a few things; I will put you in charge of many things. *Share your master's joy.*'

"The man with two talents also approached. He said, 'Master, you gave me two talents. See, I've earned two more talents.'

"His master said to him, 'Well done, good and faithful servant! You were faithful over a few things; I will put you in charge of many things. Share your master's joy.'" (Matt. 25:14–23, emphasis mine)

Whenever Missy's been gone for an afternoon adventure with Aunt Kylie and Uncle Tim (the couple who keep Missy when she's not with me, who've become family to us both) and I see their car coming up the hill that leads to our house, I usually race to the door and run out of the house to greet them. Often, Missy and I meet halfway up the walk where she jumps into my arms and we twirl around laughing. Or she takes off across the yard squealing while glancing mischievously over her shoulder at me, fully expecting me to chase her for a raucous reunion romp that often ends with me catching her and us falling into a giggling heap in the grass. Even if she's only been gone a few hours, I'm always *glad* to see her again. Usually running-toward-her-grinning-from-ear-to-ear glad. And that's the picture Jesus paints of what to expect as we march toward glory. The redemptive reality that our Savior died to provide for us is not simply for an abundant life here on this broken planet but also for an infinitely better still eternal life with a *happy* heavenly Father. Thankfully, the fact that our Creator is perfectly holy does not mean He's a severe, unsmiling grump! Because, I mean really, how could we possibly look forward to spending forever flinging crowns like Frisbees toward a grimacing, Scrooge-ish kind of King?

———

As a grade-school kid, I took the warnings from the older kids in our neighborhood very seriously. I had been warned about going near the Spanish-styled house tucked into the bend of our street. Word got around that the elderly woman occasionally seen roaming behind those gauzy curtains was a witch. She'd been known to kill small children and eat them, hiding their bones in her overgrown, side-yard fishpond. You can probably imagine my horror one day when my little brother broke free of my grasp and ran straight toward that infamous watery graveyard to see if there were any "fishies" in it.

I ran after him hissing, *"John Price, come back here right now!"* But he gleefully reached the pond before me and turned around with a triumphant smirk just about the time the side door of the haunted house creaked open and a very wrinkled, very petite lady appeared. I don't remember what her first words to us were— there was so much blood rushing through my panicked head that I couldn't hear anything else over the internal static that occurs when you assume you and your mischievous sibling are about to be cannibalized—but what she did next is tattooed on my heart. She floated graciously across her no-longer-well-kept lawn and said, "I don't get too many guests here anymore and I would sure love some company. May I offer you and your little brother some cookies or maybe a slice of cake?" That formerly dreaded neighbor's home soon became a safe harbor for my brother and me. No matter how hot and sticky we were or what time of day we rang her doorbell, Mrs. Johnson would graciously usher us into her perfectly appointed living room, serve us sweets on real china, and pleasantly engage us in conversation as if we were her favorite ladies who lunch.

To be endeared by someone you feared is a wonderfully discombobulating event. It has the power to upset your equilibrium in the best of ways, which is how I felt after reading in the whisper-thin pages of God-breathed, inscripturated truth that our Redeemer is a *happy* God. That it's okay for us to imagine Him hustling down the front steps of heaven's porch to greet us with open arms when we drive up. Or Him winking when He spots us across a crowded room and then smiling in obvious delight as He makes a beeline straight for us. Or maybe even chuckling with familial affection when rhythm-challenged followers like me are worshipping with our hands raised and eyes closed in church and invariably crash into whoever has the misfortune of standing beside us!

I was beginning to imagine God with a smiling countenance much more than a stern one.

My biblical quest to ascertain if we can accurately describe God as happy unearthed yet another scriptural diamond I'd missed previously, and it's rooted in the triune nature of our Maker. A friend of mine overheard her little girl say this to another little girl in the park recently: "I think God is more better because He's a triple!" I can't think of a better way to say it myself; our Maker's a "triple"—a Trinitarian God (Gen. 1:26–27). He exists as God the *Father*, God the *Son*, and God the *Holy Spirit*. And while Trinitarian theology can be hard to wrap our minds around, it boils down to these basic points:

1. God exists in three persons.
2. Each person is fully God.
3. There is only one God.

Clear as mud, right? Let me share a fancy term that I think may help clarify the Trinity; the term *ontological equality* means that God the Father, God the Son (Jesus), and God the Spirit are equal in value but different in function. God the Father *planned* redemption and sent His Son, Jesus, into the world to save it (John 3:16); Jesus, the Son of God, *accomplished* redemption by living a perfect, sinless life and then dying on Calvary to pay the price for the sins of mankind (John 6:38); and then after Jesus died, was resurrected, and ascended into heaven, God the Father sent the Holy Spirit to *affirm* redemption and *empower* those who put their hope in Jesus (John 14:26).

God *planned* redemption; Jesus *accomplished* redemption; and the Holy Spirit *affirms* redemption and *empowers* believers.

Furthermore, *God is a perfect community unto Himself.* At the beginning of biblical history (Gen. 1:26–27), He even refers to Himself as an "us"! In other words, God the Father, God the

Son, and God the Spirit are a *perfect* small group! They are perfectly connected. Perfectly harmonious. Perfectly balanced. Their symbiosis is supernatural and all-sufficient, which takes us to the second jewel I just mentioned:

God's happiness is entirely *self-generated and self-sustained*.

God the Father, God the Son, and God the Spirit don't have a hole to fill in their holy family. Never has one of them secretly mused, "Man, I wish We could recruit somebody else to hang out with Us because I'm getting a little tired of these Two's same old stories." They don't have personality differences or conflict that could be resolved by adding a new face to their omniscient gang.

Are you beginning to see it? If you are still a bit hesitant about this whole happy God concept, I discovered His autonomous delight is proven in both Old and New Testaments.

For instance, a familiar prophecy in Isaiah that's typically referenced with regard to the merciful way Jesus acts toward sinners also depicts God delighting in His Son. Essentially, Jehovah is smiling at Jesus, who has yet to make His incarnate earthly debut in Bethlehem:

"This is my servant; I strengthen him,
    this is my chosen one; *I delight in him*.
I have put my Spirit on him;
    he will bring justice to the nations.

He will not cry out or shout
> or make his voice heard in the streets.

He will not break a bruised reed,
> and he will not put out a smoldering wick;
> he will faithfully bring justice.

He will not grow weak or be discouraged
> until he has established justice on earth.

The coasts and islands will wait for his instruction."
(Isa. 42:1–4, emphasis mine)

Then, at the end of Jesus' High Priestly Prayer in John 17, He smiles back at His Dad while remembering their connection and mutual affection:

> "I pray not only for these, but also for those who believe in me through their word. *May they all be one, as you, Father, are in me and I am in you.* May they also be in *us*, so that the world may believe you sent me. I have given them the glory you have given me, so that *they may be one as we are one.* I am in them and you are in me, so that they may be made completely one, that the world may know you have sent me and have loved them *as you have loved me.*
>
> "Father, I want those you have given me to be with me where I am, so that they will see my glory, which you have given me because *you loved me before the world's foundation.* Righteous Father, the world has not known you. However,

I have known you, and they have known that you sent me. I made your name known to them and will continue to make it known, *so that the love you have loved me with* may be in them and I may be in them." (vv. 20–26, emphasis mine)

And then there's the time God basically breaks out in a happy dance at His only Son's baptism service:

Jesus then appeared, arriving at the Jordan River from Galilee. He wanted John to baptize him. John objected, "I'm the one who needs to be baptized, not *you!*" But Jesus insisted. "Do it. God's work, putting things right all these centuries, is coming together right now in this baptism." So John did it. The moment Jesus came up out of the baptismal waters, the skies opened up and he saw God's Spirit—it looked like a dove—descending and landing on him. And along with the Spirit, a voice: *"This is my Son, chosen and marked by my love, delight of my life."* (Matt. 3:13–17 MSG, emphasis mine)

I can totally imagine this scene because baptisms at our church are enthusiastic, celebratory affairs wherein dads often accompany their children in the baptismal pool (or into the river that runs behind our rural church property). Then our entire faith community hoots and hollers for every single redeemed sinner who gets dunked and comes bursting up out of that bath shaking sacramental drops from their hair and grinning a mile wide! But let me tell you, no one grins bigger than the mama and daddy of those dunkees. And so it is with Father God because He delights fully in His Son, Jesus, as does the Holy Spirit, who heartily echoes Jehovah's sentiment in the form of a dove. The sovereign, celebratory joy of our triune Redeemer permeates this scene, and I can't help but wonder if John the Baptist (whom Scripture depicts to be more of a sober, severe fellow, what with all the desert isolation, bug consumption, and fire and brimstone sermons) wasn't completely disconcerted by God's booming proclamation of parental joy!

Much like John, the reality of a perfectly happy—perhaps even boisterous—triune God may be somewhat disconcerting for you too. It seems to rattle the cage of orthodoxy a tad, doesn't it? May I be so bold as to encourage, even *challenge* you, to invite the Holy Spirit to mess with your mental image of God? I can pretty well promise you that you'll be glad you did.

The Practical Pursuit of Happiness

1. Is there a Bible story or scenario in which you can imagine God the Father or Jesus the Son smiling? If so, please explain.

_____

_____

_____

2. How has your experience of human fatherhood colored your perception of God the Father (please feel free to share positive and/or negative impressions)?

_____

_____

_____

3. What part of John Piper's quote on pages 24 and 25 resonates most with you? Was any part of his assertion revelatory or "news" to you? If so, please explain.

_____

_____

_____

4. When—if ever—have you sensed God moving toward you with a smile?

_____

_____

_____

5. Have you ever been endeared by someone you initially feared? If so, please explain.

_____

_____

_____

6. How would you paraphrase Matthew 3:17 (God's response after John the Baptist "dunked" Jesus!)?

_____

_____

_____

7. How do you think you could benefit spiritually from inviting the Holy Spirit to mess with your mental image of God?

_____

_____

_____

Is God Happy with Me?

*As there is the most heat nearest to the sun, so
is the most happiness nearest to Christ.*
Charles Spurgeon

I'M NOT SURE HOW TO PUT THIS DELICATELY, NOR DO I
want to alarm those of you who are currently enjoying the
vibrant, highly metabolic stage of early adulthood. But alas, I am
not. Instead, I'm in my mostly content, well-earned, middle-aged
season of life, which also means my body is currently toying with
me as it . . . ummm, *pauses* certain previous functions. And I'm
at the age and stage of wildly enthusiastic perspiration. My dis-
loyal lady parts leapfrogged right over innocuous hot flashes and

have chosen to participate in a lesser-known menopausal symptom called "volcanic eruptions." In other words, I sweat like a sumo wrestler in a sauna and typically do so at very inopportune times. Like at public functions when I'm speaking or at four o'clock in the morning when I should be sleeping.

Such was the case a few weeks ago when I woke up before dawn, wide-eyed and disoriented, only to discover I was essentially floating in a pool of my own making. I groggily thought, *Okay, I can either lie here and let my frustration grow with each soggy passing second, or I can go ahead and get up and pray earnestly that my emotions and mental faculties will choose* not *to conspire with my ovaries and completely betray me. On second thought,* I mused, *maybe a cup of super-hot coffee could trick my body into cooling down.* This compelled me to roll out of bed and stumble through the dark to the pantry rooting for java beans.

I found just enough in the bottom of a bag to French-press one single cup of deliciousness. Steaming cup of joy in hand, I was ready to savor my coffee in peace at the kitchen island while watching the sun come up. But when I went to sit down on the barstool, I slipped (Thank you, perspiration!) on the edge of it and accidentally spilled my coffee all over papers that were spread out on the island. The ruined paperwork was none other than Missy's homeschool lesson for the day. In that moment, I made the executive decision to move our schoolwork to the mall for a little lesson on capitalism. And I was pretty sure Jesus was okay with us driving through Starbucks en route.

When she woke up a few hours later, I informed Missy of our edited plans with lots of positivity and bundled her into the car to race for caffeine before she had time to balk. Unfortunately, the barista mirrored my morning and grumpily passed my extra-hot, nonfat mocha with whip (I stand by my conviction that the nonfat milk and whipped cream cancel each other out, making my drink choice almost healthy) through the drive-thru window with a sniff of condescension. In my opinion, young men wearing cropped pants have abdicated the right to be condescending, but I digress.

Anyway, I'm pretty sure Mr. Disdainful Short Pants *meant* to hand me a cup with an unsecured lid that would inevitably spill when I took it from him. I don't know how you react when you've already endured a very bad, no good, horrible morning and then a cup of boiling coffee sloshes into your lap, but I blurted a word that's not in the Bible. I'm not proud of it, but alas, that's what I did.

Now, since English is Missy's second language, she developed a habit soon after I brought her home from Haiti of weaving new words into song melodies because that helped her remember them. And within a nanosecond she wove that bad word into her current favorite tune, which is Chris Tomlin's "Good, Good Father." Within another nanosecond, I dug my pit of sin even deeper with the transgression of deception. "Oh, no, baby," I whirled around and said, "*that's* not the word Mama said! Mama said . . . (at which point I sang these words to the same worship tune she'd just innocently warbled), 'You're a good, good coffee cup. So *sit* right here, *sit* right here.'" Picture this scene with me exaggerating the motion of taking the cup from the drive-thru window and placing it in the front-seat cup holder. By the time we pulled into the Dillard's parking lot, I felt like the worst Christ-following mom on the planet because before it was even lunchtime, my child had skipped school, heard me blurt a bad word, and then unwittingly participated in song piracy!

Moments like those remind me how desperate I am for divine grace. It's also moments like those that prompt me to wonder how in the world a perfect God could possibly be happy with *me*. I mean, good night, we've already established that His joy is self-sufficient, that our triune Redeemer doesn't need human interaction to be happy. So where does that leave us, especially those of us who are prone to wander, don't fill in every Bible study blank, and sometimes lead their precious children into truancy?

In *The Pleasures of God*, John Piper's wisdom guided me toward a theologically sound answer to the question "Is God happy with me?" My dog-eared copy of his book contains a passage I underlined more than ten years ago that still encourages my spirit:

> God does what he does, not begrudgingly or under external constraint as though he were boxed in or trapped by some unforeseen or unplanned situation. On the contrary,

because he is complete and exuberantly happy and overflowing with satisfaction in the fellowship of the Trinity,
all he does is free and uncoerced.[1]

If you marinate in Piper's statement long enough, I can
almost guarantee your soul will begin to shift toward relief and
maybe even exultation. While God doesn't *need* us to be happy,
He *chooses* to include us in His joy.

Apostle Paul put it this way in Ephesians:

Because of his love, God had already decided to make us
his own children through Jesus Christ. *That was what he
wanted and what pleased him* . . . (Eph. 1:5 NCV, emphasis
mine)

Centuries before the prophet Isaiah put it like this:

"Remember the former things long past,
For I am God, and there is no other;
I am God, and there is no one like Me,
Declaring the end from the beginning,
And from ancient times things which have not been done,
Saying, 'My purpose will be established,
And I will accomplish all My good pleasure . . .'"
(Isa. 46:9–10 NASB, emphasis mine)

Is this as enlightening to you as it is to me? When I read the
above passage in Isaiah now, it's as if the Holy Spirit nudges me

with a wink, and this truth He's been whispering to my spirit for decades swells into a beautiful chorus that I can't help but hear!

———

Growing up, I spent a few weeks every summer at this wonderful place in Central Florida called Lake Swan Camp. Lake Rosa, the smaller pond, bordered the camp on the south side while the bigger pond called Lake Swan (hence the camp's name) bordered on the north. My fingers often resembled prunes when I was a camper because we spent so much time in the water skiing and swimming and sailing! When we weren't in the water, we were frolicking on the soccer field or eating hot fudge sundaes as big as our heads in the snack shack. And every night we had worship in the chapel with two or three darling surfer dudes playing guitars, followed by some engaging youth pastor encouraging us to run hard toward Jesus.

Lake Swan Camp. Where I learned to barefoot water ski and play Capture the Flag. Where I learned to run boys' briefs up the flagpole and study the Bible. Where I learned to begin my day with Jesus (which was necessary in light of all that running of boys' undies up the flagpole the night before). It was my teenage happy place . . . except for one nerve-racking hour every summer when all campers were forced to participate in something called the Sadie Hawkins Day Race.

I don't know if you observed Sadie Hawkins–themed events when you were growing up, but recently I discovered that Sadie wasn't even a real person. She originated in the syndicated comic strip *Li'l Abner*. And for some reason, at least when I was younger, events in Sadie's honor typically involved some type of comical gender role reversal, and our Christian church camp was no different. All the girl campers chased the boy campers to "catch" their date for the big end-of-camp banquet.

Picture it . . . every year the counselors would call all of us to the field in front of Lake Rosa and line us up—all the girls on one side of the field and all the boys across from us with their backs to the lake. About 200 teenage girls standing shoulder to shoulder faced the lake and about 150 anxious, mostly prepubescent boys effectively trapped on the beach! Upon hearing the head counselor's whistle, all the girls took off like they were shot out of a cannon to catch the boy who would be their date later that evening at the Sadie Hawkins dance.

Sometimes I wonder who came up with this sadistic idea, if some of those poor boys needed therapy as grown men, and whether or not some of the girls struggled with submission "issues" later on in life! Furthermore, our Sadie Hawkins dance was never a real dance. Lake Swan was owned and operated by a very conservative denomination, and the powers that be decided that God-fearing teenagers were not allowed to boogie on the property. We all just stood around the cafeteria fidgeting in our dress clothes during the "dance." However, the "dance" was still the grand finale of two weeks at camp, so the question, "Who are you going to chase?" was the most commonly whispered question in the girls' cabins, and we anxiously plotted chasing strategies during free time.

The summer I turned fifteen, Jeff McGarvey was the guy almost *every* girl secretly hoped to catch at the Sadie Hawkins race. Jeff had curly brown hair and a killer jump shot. The guys all admired his basketball skills while we girls all admired his legs. He was a real Hottie-McTottie. A few minutes before the race that Thursday in August 1979, he knocked on the door of our cabin and asked if I'd come outside so he could ask me something. Of course, his appearance at our threshold sent all my cabinmates into a titter of giggles and whispers. I was embarrassed by all the commotion but wasn't flustered about Jeff; I'd known him since childhood. And because we lived in the same hometown, I assumed he was going to ask if my parents could give him a ride home from camp the next day. But when we walked outside together, I noticed his nervousness; how he was scuffing the toe of his Chuck Taylor's in the dirt and his neck was covered in red splotches.

He hemmed and hawed for a while, then flashed me a shy smile and said, "I think it'd be cool to go to the dance with you tonight. So if you think that's cool too, after they blow the whistle, run over to the place between the boys' cabins and the snack shop, and I'll get there as fast as I can to let you tag me." I don't remember my reply verbatim, but it was basically, "Okay, cool." I do, however, remember the moments that followed. I remember it was really hot as we all stood in opposing Sadie Hawkins lines. I remember the other girls were fanning themselves and gossiping about who they were going to chase. I remember that when the head counselor blew the whistle I was the only girl who didn't take off running. I stood there smiling and watched at least twenty girls make a beeline for Jeff.

I watched him zig and zag and easily evade even the most determined of his pursuers for a minute or two. Then I turned and trotted over toward the snack shack. And, sure enough, moments later, Jeff came racing up through the woods and skidded to a stop right in front of me. Then I reached out and tagged him. That night I wore a peach, Quiana knit dress with spaghetti straps, and Jeff wore a light-blue, polyester leisure suit with a vest, and I felt like a queen on the arm of her king! I smiled so wide for so long throughout our boogie-less dance in the cafeteria that night, my cheeks started to cramp. All I could think was, _He. Picked. Me!_

Sometimes I wonder if I have such fond memories of that night thirty-five years ago because it's one of the last really good dates I've experienced. I'm kidding . . . mostly! In reality, I smiled until my face hurt then and still smile at the memory of that long-ago Sadie Hawkins "dance" now because I was chosen. This is the point Piper makes in his book and Paul and Isaiah make in The Book: _God chose us._ The King of all kings, who is perfectly content, fulfilled, and self-sufficiently happy, _chooses_ to include us in His glorious joy. He leaned down from glory not because He needs us but because He *wants* to be with us. He picked us to be part of His good pleasure.

Furthermore, Jeff's biggest sacrifice in letting me know he was keen to go to the Sadie Hawkins dance with me was a short jog over to the girls' cabins; God's pursuit of us came at an immeasurably higher price. It required sending His only Son to be crushed so that we could be saved:

> He made the one who did not know sin to be sin for us, so that in him we might become the righteousness of God. (2 Cor. 5:21)

> If God didn't hesitate to put everything on the line for us, embracing our condition and exposing himself to the worst by sending his own Son, is there anything else he wouldn't gladly and freely do for us? (Rom. 8:32 MSG)

There's a lovely dissonance between being needed and being *wanted*. Being needed puts the onus squarely on us, on our continued performance, ability, and usefulness. But being *wanted* puts the onus on God, on His sovereign choice to redeem us through the death and resurrection of Jesus and then to adopt us into His forever family when we put our hope and belief in what He sacrificed and accomplished on our behalf.

I had two failed adoption attempts prior to Missy, so to say my heart was plowed up is an understatement. Frankly, my heart felt like roadkill that kept getting pulverized by bigger and bigger trucks. So early on, when I met with another adoptive mom who'd already brought her HIV-positive child home from a Third World country and she told me she often found herself wishing she had HIV, I didn't have the emotional bandwidth to understand exactly what she meant by that. I assumed she meant she'd be more than willing to suffer with the virus if that meant her baby wouldn't have to—kind of a quid pro quo penitential parenting kind of thing. Or maybe she was just being overly emotional and hyperbolic as mamas sometimes are when it comes to our children.

It wasn't until two years later—a few days after I'd wept through the customs line in Miami while holding Missy's hand because the reality hit me that she was officially my daughter after twenty-four roller-coaster months of slogging through seemingly endless paperwork, the maddeningly slow Haitian child welfare system, and worrying about her physical and emotional health from two thousand miles away—when I held her while she screamed throughout the first of what will be a lifetime of blood draws—that I finally understood. Because even though she'd only been a U.S. citizen for a few days at that point in April 2014, she'd been my baby girl since the first time I held her in

April 2012; covered in scabies, her tiny lungs filled with fluid from tuberculosis, her body frail from malnutrition, her hair reddened by the lack of nutrients in what little food she was getting, and her baby teeth brown from lack of care and hygiene. By the time I brought her home, I knew the way her eyelids got heavy during her favorite bedtime lullabies, the way she wiggled and bounced when she was excited, the fierce resolve in her eyes when she was determined, and the tone of her sobs when she was truly heartbroken. Two years after they'd placed a wary nineteen-pound toddler in my arms, she was wholly and completely *my kid*.

I sat on the edge of the pleather chair in the phlebotomist's office, firmly hugging and rocking my panicky Haitian daughter and whispering in her ear, "It's going to be okay, baby. This is going to sting, but it'll be over quickly. I'm so sorry, honey. *Mwen se konsa regrèt.*" And I thought, *Now, I get it. I can totally understand what my friend meant by saying she wished she had HIV like her child because I am so connected with Missy, I want to be able to feel what she feels. I want to empathize with her and comfort her so she will never feel alone, no matter what the situation. Every. Single. Thing. That concerns her, concerns me.*

Infinitely more than I am bonded to my precious child, God the Father is perfectly bound with His Son, Jesus. Whatever concerns Jesus, concerns Him. Therefore, if you've put your hope and faith in Jesus, God is happy with you because He's utterly and absolutely happy with His Son. Just listen to the joyful proclamation Jesus makes in John's gospel account concerning this very issue:

> *"As the Father has loved me, so have I loved you.* Abide in my love. If you keep my commandments, you will abide in my love, just as I have kept my Father's commandments and abide in his love. These things I have spoken to you, *that my joy may be in you, and that your joy may be full.* This is my commandment, that you love one another as I have loved you. Greater love has no one than this, that someone lay down his life for his friends. You are my friends if you do what I command you. *No longer do I call you servants, for the servant does not know what his master is doing; but I have called you friends, for all that I have heard from my Father I have made known to you. You did not choose me, but I chose you* and appointed you that you should go and bear fruit and that your fruit should abide, so that *whatever you ask the Father in my name, he may give it to you."* (John 15:9–16 ESV, emphasis mine)

And just in case you're like me and tend to be thick as a brick when it comes to understanding your identity in Christ, here are a few more passages echoing Jesus' promise from John 15:

> For through faith you are all sons of God in Christ Jesus. For those of you who were baptized into Christ have been clothed with Christ. (Gal. 3:26–27)

Now you are no longer a slave but God's own child. And since you are his child, God has made you his heir. (Gal. 4:7 NLT)

You did not receive a spirit of slavery to fall back into fear. Instead, you received the Spirit of adoption, by whom we cry out, "Abba, Father!" The Spirit himself testifies together with our spirit that we are God's children, and if children, also heirs—heirs of God and coheirs with Christ—if indeed we suffer with him so that we may also be glorified with him. (Rom. 8:15–17)

See what great love the Father has lavished on us, that we should be called children of God! And that is what we are! (1 John 3:1a NIV)

———

As heartwarming as my Sadie Hawkins experience was in my teens, I've had a few dating experiences since that were much less so. One of my biggest crushes in my twenties was a lothario I'll call Absalom for the sake of his anonymity (and he *was* really fastidious about his hair). Anyway, Ab and I did the post-college, almost-dating thing for more than a year, which meant we hung out all the time, practiced safe flirting, attended lots of social gatherings as a couple, and never kissed. But things seemed to be taking a turn toward romantic when he asked me out for Valentine's Day and took me to a very nice restaurant. After the waiter cleared the table and took our dessert order, Ab excused himself for a few minutes, then came striding back toward me carrying a large, beautifully wrapped box and grinning like a Cheshire cat.

I was flustered because I hadn't brought a gift for him—it's awkward when you're in a "plating" (platonic-dating) relationship because things like gift-giving parameters aren't clear—but he brushed that off with a sly grin and said, "Go ahead, open it!" So I carefully peeled the exquisite paper off and opened the box to find a gorgeous, extremely expensive dress. Now, I was really flustered because not only was it the first time a guy bought me a dress, but the tag revealed it was two sizes too small. His eyes got all shiny with excitement as he asked me repeatedly if I liked it. After telling him that the dress was lovely—albeit too expensive—and that I really appreciated his generosity, he asked if I wanted to try it on. Of course, I demurred since we were, after all, in a restaurant. But because he insisted, I had to spill the beans and tell him it was too small.

He then leaned forward and said smoothly and sincerely, "Lisa, I knew it was too small when I bought it. Here's the deal, there's a line between pretty and beautiful, and I think you're about ten or fifteen pounds away from it. But I really want to fall in love with you, so I bought you this dress as an incentive. As soon as you can fit into it, I'm sure we'll be able to make a go of it." The fifty-three-year-old me would've had the self-respect to say, "Oh well. Your loss, Pea-brain," and then turn, walk out of the restaurant, and Uber home. But twenty-three-year-old me just sat there feeling my face get hot and wishing I'd ordered a salad as my entree.

Here's the liberating truth about God being happy with us: it's not up to us! We don't have to work harder to make it into some elusive "I deserve to be happy" club. We can't instigate or impel divine happiness, nor can we lose or lessen divine happiness. God's joy is self-generated and sustained with and through His Spirit and His Son. So when we put our trust in Jesus and receive the accompanying infilling of the Holy Spirit, we become heirs of His divine delight. We are grafted in, so to speak, chosen to be the apple of God's eye and beneficiaries of His good pleasure.

You and I are *so* getting the long end of the stick in this delight deal.

The Practical Pursuit of Happiness

1. How and when does your insecurity regarding God's unconditional affection for you typically show up?

When I think of how bad I do
w/ consistent devotions sometimes

2. When and where did you first begin to believe that God *chose* you?

_____

_____

_____

3. How would you explain the difference between *needing* to be with someone and *wanting* to be with someone?

Need is out of obligation -unhealthy?

Want is out of desire

_____

4. Reread Romans 8:32. How would you paraphrase this verse in personal language?

_____

_____

_____

5. Are you more prone to linger in the embrace of someone safe or wriggle out of it as soon as possible?

Linger

_____

_____

6. Do you feel comfortable lingering in God's affection for you? If so, please describe the most recent "embrace" you enjoyed with Him.

_____

_____

_____

7. If you answered yes to the above question, what does an "embrace" with God look and feel like for you?

_____

_____

_____

CHAPTER FOUR

How Do You Get Happy?

*Love then, and be happy, beloved children of my heart!
And never forget, that until the day God will deign
to reveal the future to man, <u>all human wisdom is
contained in these two words</u>—"Wait and Hope."*
Alexandre Dumas

BLOODWORK IS THE BANE OF MY DAUGHTER'S EXISTENCE. Missy's totally unfazed by normal childhood fears like boogie men or broccoli, but goodness help you if you're anywhere near us and aren't wearing earphones when my child gets the quarterly blood draws to monitor her HIV. Her shrieks are loud enough to shatter the windows. Or eardrums. Honestly, my sweet girl's needle phobia is justified. She got jabbed way too many times by rushed, gruff, and/or inexperienced technicians in Haiti; more than once when I visited her during our adoption process her little arms were bruised and swollen because of inept medical care. Of course, we've worked on managing her situational anxiety for a long time and have tried everything our wonderful doctor and nurse suggested; we read several books written specifically to desensitize kids to medical procedures, role-played the routine with Missy taking a turn as the "nice" phlebotomist, did site massage, processed it ad-nauseam verbally, and tried numerous other techniques that typically work with children. All to no avail.

So I decided to go old-school and simple at her last hospital visit. When the nurse came out and called Missy's name, signaling that it was time for us to go to the lab for her blood draw, she began to panic. I squatted down to her level, held her trembling shoulders, and said, "Baby, all you have to do is focus on me this time instead of Miss Sandy's needle and it won't be as scary. It'll sting for just a second, and then it'll be over. Just focus on me, honey . . . You look in my eyes and everything will be okay, I promise." It was all I could do not to cry when she let out a shuddering exhale and put her hand in mine for the long walk back to the dreaded "poking room."

Missy began to cry softly and squirm when the nurse started the familiar routine of wrapping a rubber tourniquet around her bicep and swabbing the crook of her elbow with alcohol. Gently but firmly I kept repeating, "Look at me, honey. Don't look at Miss Sandy—look at Mama. Look at me, baby." And just before

Sandy plunged that surgical steel barb in my baby's arm, Missy turned to me with her big brown eyes brimming with tears. Instantaneously, an avalanche of affection welled up in me, and my voice caught as I murmured, "Keep looking at me, baby. I've got you. Everything's going to be okay." As I thought to myself, *This is one of the sweetest, most vulnerable moments we've ever shared,* Missy sat up a little straighter with an alarmed look on her face and declared loudly, "Mama, you have a Big. Black. Hair. Coming out of your chin!"

While I didn't anticipate this precious exchange with my daughter ending with me making an appointment for laser hair removal, I was delighted that my unwanted whisker gave Missy a much-needed reprieve from her fear. Plus, I'm a firm believer that being able to laugh at yourself is one of the key components to consistent happiness.

In his best-selling book, *Flourish,* psychologist Dr. Martin Seligman encourages readers with five other key components of life to achieve happiness and well-being:

1. Positive emotion
2. Engagement
3. Positive relationships
4. Meaning
5. Achievement[1]

In Gretchen Rubin's *New York Times* best seller, *The Happiness Project*, she chose these twelve "resolutions"—one for each month of the year—to work on:

1. Vitality (January)
2. Marriage (February)
3. Work (March)
4. Parenthood (April)
5. Leisure (May)
6. Friendship (June)
7. Money (July)
8. Eternity (August)
9. Books (September)
10. Mindfulness (October)
11. Attitude (November)
12. Happiness (December)

Then she came up with these twelve principles or "commandments" by which to keep her resolutions:

1. Be Gretchen.
2. Let it go.
3. Act the way I want to feel.
4. Do it now.
5. Be polite and be fair.
6. Enjoy the process.
7. Spend out.
8. Identify the problem.

9. Lighten up.

10. Do what ought to be done.

11. No calculation.

12. There is only love.[2]

Some of the practical wisdom she gleaned and generously shared as a result of her happiness project was helpful to me while I was on my own "journey of joy" research: *go to sleep earlier, take time to be silly, be generous, sing in the morning, don't gossip,* and *keep a gratitude notebook.*

Dr. Emma Seppälä—Science Director at Stanford's Center for Compassion and Altruism Research and Education and a frequent contributor to *Harvard Business Review,* as well as *Psychology Today*—recently synopsized the six keys to happiness and success as being:

1. Live (or work) in the moment.

2. Tap into your resilience.

3. Manage your energy.

4. Do nothing.

5. Be good to yourself.

6. Show compassion to others.[3]

Again, I found her advice beneficial, although as a single mom who travels for a living, I'm having a hard time mastering the *do nothing* principle!

And then there are the "Ten Practices of Happiness" that author Deborah K. Heisz and the editors of *Live Happy* magazine (yes, there is such a publication) suggest in the book *Live Happy*:

1. Attitude
2. Connection
3. Meaning
4. Creativity
5. Gratitude
6. Mindfulness
7. Health
8. Resilience
9. Spirituality
10. Giving Back[4]

I especially enjoyed some of the medically proven scaffolding of their happiness practices, such as the fact that people who count their blessings on a regular basis have fewer aches and pains and better sleep than people who focus more on life's burdens.[5] And children who had a positive outlook on life at age seven show better overall health and fewer illnesses thirty years later.[6]

However, after leafing through page after page of good practical advice in my stack of books on happiness, I couldn't help longing for a simpler "technique." So I turned to another Book and, wouldn't you know it, our happiness boils down to pretty much what I told Missy a few weeks ago at the hospital: "Focus on me, baby. Focus on me." Only the parent urging us to look at Him is perfect.

———

Without knowing you, there's a good chance that whether you're churched or unchurched you're familiar with the story of the good Samaritan. Regardless of whether one recognizes the deity of the Storyteller, just about everyone can recognize the merit of its humanitarian theme. But if you'll dig a little deeper, you'll also find the "How-To's" of happy; so go ahead, please, peruse this familiar story again.

> Then an expert in the law stood up to test him, saying, "Teacher, what must I do to inherit eternal life?"
>
> "What is written in the law?" he asked him. "How do you read it?"
>
> He answered, "Love the Lord your God with all your heart, with all your soul, with all your strength, and with all your mind;" and "your neighbor as yourself."
>
> "You've answered correctly," he told him. "Do this and you will live."
>
> But wanting to justify himself, he asked Jesus, "And who is my neighbor?"
>
> Jesus took up the question and said: "A man was going down *from Jerusalem to Jericho* and fell into the hands of robbers. They stripped him, beat him up, and

fled, leaving him half dead. A priest happened to be going down that road. When he saw him, he passed by on the other side. In the same way, a Levite, when he arrived at the place and saw him, passed by on the other side. But a Samaritan on his journey came up to him, and when he saw the man, he had compassion. He went over to him and bandaged his wounds, pouring on olive oil and wine. Then he put him on his own animal, brought him to an inn, and took care of him. The next day he took out two denarii, gave them to the innkeeper, and said, 'Take care of him. When I come back I'll reimburse you for whatever extra you spend.'

"Which of these three do you think proved to be a neighbor to the man who fell into the hands of the robbers?"

"The one who showed mercy to him," he said.

(Luke 10:25–37, emphasis mine)

The Hebraic teaching style of the good Samaritan is called *Proem Midrash*, and it means, "let our master teach us." This may help elucidate its Socrates-type format of asking and answering questions. The first query posed to Jesus—*What must I do to inherit eternal life?*—was done so by an uppity attorney. Then the Messiah parried with one of His own: *What does the law say?* Of course, the King of all kings knew this condescending barrister had memorized the Torah and wasn't surprised when he answered correctly by quoting from Deuteronomy (6:5) and from Leviticus (19:18). But then

Jesus threw down the gauntlet by commanding him to practice what he proclaimed: *Do this and you will live.*

The lawyer's pride now reared its hideous head. Because if he'd truly considered the directive and replied honestly, he would've said something like, "Sir, I haven't loved God with all my heart, soul, mind, and strength. And I haven't loved my neighbors very well either. As a matter of fact, one of my neighbors gets on my last nerve because there's an old car stacked on cement blocks in their front yard. Plus, they slammed the door in my kid's face when she was selling Girl Scout cookies."

He should've both admitted to the fact that he couldn't possibly fulfill all 613 laws of the Torah and acknowledged that he was desperate for divine grace. Instead, he totally ignored the first command quoted and tried to employ a diversionary stall tactic. He asked Jesus a trivial question about the second command: *And just what exactly do you mean by the word* neighbor? Rather than rebuking the guy or frying him into a grease spot of oblivion, Jesus gently put him in his place by sharing a vivid example of what love looks like, and in so doing, underscored the parameters of happy. Please hang with me while we look deeper at the key details in these verses together since understanding the context of the story will help illuminate those parameters.

First, the road discussed here was dangerous. It was a winding, rocky path that descended almost 3,500 feet in seventeen miles. Additionally, because it had such a bad reputation for criminal activity, people called it "The Way of Blood." Second, it's significant that the priest's and the Levite's particular journey on this infamous road was taking them *from* Jerusalem *to* Jericho. This detail implies that they were headed home from their cubicles in the temple to their homes in the suburbs.

The priest had probably been burning incense and offering sacrifices all week long. He'd presided over legal cases and he'd blessed babies. Levites were subordinate to priests in temple hierarchy, but he, too, had been working hard all week assisting in the traditions of temple worship. They'd been very busy and very visible working for Jehovah. But now they were on their way home to relax. Maybe watch a little JSPN, the Jerusalem Sports Network, or do a little fishing. Obviously, I'm taking some liberty with the Greek here, but what's important for us to understand is where these two have been and where they're going.

It's also important to note there's a ceremonial law that states that anyone who touches a dead body shall be rendered unclean for seven days. Because it's often taught that the priest and the Levite might not have stopped to help the man in the ditch because they feared being unclean. However, Luke's directional specification about them walking *from* Jerusalem *to* Jericho makes that a moot point because whatever ritual purity they may have been protecting because of their responsibilities in the temple didn't really matter since they were headed home from work.

While the priest and the Levite had fulfilled their Torah obligations—they kept the *letter* of the law—they missed the whole point of loving God and other people. By focusing on religion instead of relationships, they forfeited a great shot at happiness. My guess is the only joyful person in this parable is the Samaritan, whom you may remember was from a people group judged by the Jews to be worse than the gum stuck to the bottom of their sandals. This is another key piece to understanding the full context of this story. Jews absolutely despised Samaritans. These two people groups didn't just march to the beat of a different drum; they hurled bricks at the opposing drumline!

The animosity between Jews and Samaritans began 750 years before the earthly life and ministry of Jesus Christ. A violent people group called the Assyrians conquered the northern kingdom of Israel where Samaria is located. The result was a country where Jews and Assyrians intermarried; typically, an Assyrian man took a Jewish wife—among his many other wives—in order to further subjugate the Jews and weaken their bloodlines. Their descendents came to be known as Samaritans—people who were half Jewish and half Assyrians and were vilified as impure traitors by Orthodox Jews.

The battle lines only grew deeper over the years. For instance, when the southern Jews returned to Jerusalem after the Babylonian captivity and began to rebuild the temple, the Samaritans offered to help. The Jews said, "No thanks, you bunch of dirty half-breeds." So the Samaritans said, "Fine, you bunch of stuck-up nerds, we'll build our own temple on Mount Gerizim." (Again, I'm taking just a teensy bit of liberty with the nuances of their dialogue, but you get the gist.) The Samaritans went on to establish their own priesthood, independent of the Jews, and considered only the first five books of the Torah—the Pentateuch—to be authoritative, while observant Jews revered the entire compilation of the Law—the Historical Books, the Wisdom Books, and the Prophets. Essentially, Samaritans disregarded everything Jews held sacred, and the Jews fumed to the point of cursing their Samaritan neighbors publicly in the synagogue and praying for Jehovah to exclude them from eternal life.

In fact, just one chapter earlier in Luke's Gospel account, an entire Samaritan village had rejected Jesus, making James and John so mad they asked the Lamb of God if they could call down fire from heaven and zap them! In light of all this combative history, you would think that Jesus—being a Jew—would've made the Samaritan the bad guy in this story. Or at the very least, made him the guy in the ditch. But instead Jesus made him the hero.

The audacious moral Jesus illustrated to the surely flustered attorney that *all* people matter to God, and therefore *all* people should matter to us—especially to those of us who love God. The takeaway of this story, fulfilling the entirety of what God commands, requires loving Him and loving each other. And I hope you also see the handwriting on the wall relevant to our subject matter . . . God may as well tap us on the shoulder and whisper, *Love Me and love each other and you'll not only fulfill the law, you'll* be fulfilled. *Focus on these two things and You'll. Be. Happy.*

Not only am I striving to love God and love people, but I'm trying to instill that mind-set in Missy, too. Almost every time she and I leave the house and head to the car—whether we're going to Target or racing to the airport to travel to a conference—I ask her this question: "Honey, what is your responsibility?" And she replies, "To be kind, polite, is-is-spectful [her version of "respectful"], and have fun, Mama!" Every now and then when she asks me why, I tell her because we're Harpers and we love God. I continue to explain that four basic ways we can show other people how awesome it is to be in a relationship with God are to *be kind to all the people He created, polite to all the people He created, respectful to all the people He created, and have fun no matter where we are in His creation.*

We'd had that conversation almost verbatim last week when we left the house to travel to an event in Texas. She repeated her responsibility mantra so sweetly and confidently, my chest swelled with parental pride. I thought, *My kid has got this thing dialed in! The Harpers are cooking with gas this weekend, baby!* Less than an hour later, God pricked my smug balloon with the needle of reality when Missy and I were in adjacent stalls in the airport restroom (she's at the stage when she wants "pwi-vecie" in the potty whenever possible so I've just recently started letting her use the stall next to mine when we're out in public). All was well until the poor woman in the stall next to Missy had some very loud intestinal issues. At which point my precious daughter "whispered" loud enough for people walking by the restroom to hear, "Mama, dat lady just passed gas in pah-lick and dat's *not* polite . . . dat's trashy!"

You've never seen a mama hustle her child out of a public bathroom so fast. Missy's pants were still unzipped and her hands were dripping as I rushed toward the concourse and away from that anonymous lady she'd heaped shame upon! I realized in that moment that while our family ethics were fairly simple, I still needed to clarify *how* to best walk out those principles!

In a similar vein, Scripture clarifies what it looks like to walk out the two main biblical principles of happy—*Focus on God* first and foremost and then *Focus on Others*.

How to Focus on God

Be a Follower of Jesus Christ = Happy

"Tell us," they asked Jesus, "are you the one John said was going to come, or should we expect someone else?" Jesus answered, "Go back and tell John what you are hearing and seeing: the blind can see, the lame can walk, those who suffer from dreaded skin diseases are made clean, the deaf hear, the dead are brought back to life, and the Good News is preached to the poor. How *happy are those who have no doubts about me*!" (Matt. 11:3–6 GNT, emphasis mine)

Jesus said to him, "Thomas, because you have seen Me, you believe. *Those are happy who have never seen Me and yet believe*!" (John 20:29 NLV, emphasis mine)

Be Aware of God's Forgiveness = Happy

Happy are those whose wrongs are forgiven, whose sins are pardoned! Happy is the person whose sins the Lord will not keep account of! (Rom. 4:7–8 GNT, emphasis mine)

Be Faithful to Him Even When Life Is Hard = Happy

Happy is the person who can hold up under the trials of life. At the right time, he'll know God's sweet approval and will be crowned with life. As God has promised, the crown awaits all who love Him. (James 1:12 The Voice, emphasis mine)

Be God's Servant = Happy

"*How happy are those servants* whose master finds them awake and ready when he returns! I tell you, he will take

off his coat, have them sit down, and will wait on them."
(Luke 12:37 GNT, emphasis mine)

Be Convinced God Can Do the Impossible = Happy

Happy is she who believed that the Lord would fulfill the
promises he made to her. [The context here is Mary's belief
when Gabriel told her she was going to be the mother of
the Messiah.] (Luke 1:45 CEB, emphasis mine)

Be Obedient to God's Commandments = Happy

*But the one who keeps looking into God's perfect Law and
does not forget it will do what it says and be happy as he does
it.* God's Word makes men free. (James 1:25 NLV, emphasis
mine)

Be Alert about Christ's Return = Happy

"Listen! I am coming like a thief! *Happy is he who stays
awake* and guards his clothes, so that he will not walk
around naked and be ashamed in public!" (Rev. 16:15 GNT,
emphasis mine)

How to Focus on Others

Be Compassionate and Generous with God's Image-Bearers = Happy

> In everything I have given you an example of how, by working hard like this, you must help the weak, remembering the words of the Lord Yeshua himself, *"There is more happiness in giving than in receiving."* (Acts 20:35 CJB, emphasis mine)

I don't know about you, but as a busy chick who often has too many irons in the fire, I'm beyond grateful that God made happiness a relatively simple sacrament. Focus on Him and be kind, polite, generous, and is-is-spectful of others . . . I might just be able to handle that!

The Practical Pursuit of Happiness

1. Do you agree or disagree with the Alexandre Dumas quote at the beginning of this chapter? Please explain your answer.

   faith requires more than wait + hope — calls us to action

2. With whom are you most comfortable laughing at yourself?

    Close friends
    _____

    _____

    _____

3. Which of Dr. Seligman's five components to achieve happiness
    and well-being are you currently living out well?

    _____

    _____

    _____

4. Which of Dr. Seppälä's *6 Keys to Happiness* are you currently
    living out well?

    _____

    _____

    _____

5. How do you personally identify with each of the characters in
    the story of the good Samaritan?

    _____

    _____

    _____

6. Whom do you know who lives a God-and-others centric kind of life really well?

_____

_____

_____

7. Reread Luke 1:45. How has God proved that He can do the impossible in your life lately?

_____

_____

_____

How Does Happy Express Itself?

Happiness isn't something that depends on our surroundings—it's something we make inside ourselves.
Corrie Ten Boom

I HAVE A PRETTY HIGH ENERGY LEVEL—SOME HAVE EVEN accused me of being hyper—but man, this single motherhood gig burns a lot more gas than my pre-mom life, and sometimes I'm just flat worn-out as a result. After Missy and I had spent three days at a conference in Dallas recently, I found myself literally daydreaming about the possibility of a nap on the flight home while the hostess was driving us to the airport. I was plum giddy by the thought, *If I can just get her settled in watching a Dora movie, I could have more than an hour to snooze in the air!* Of course, as soon as we got to our gate at DFW, the American Airlines agent manning it announced that our flight was oversold and perkily exclaimed they'd give a $200 voucher to anyone willing to give up their seat and take the next flight to Nashville, which departed the following morning. When not enough people responded to the bribe, he resorted to begging. As much as I felt sorry for him, I was resolute. There was no way I was going to give up our seats when a potential nap was at stake.

When finally boarding the plane, I discovered we'd been moved to the second to the last row because of a booking error. I reasoned, "Row 172 has the same seats as Row 12; perfect for sleeping!" When we schlepped our stuff all the way to the back of the plane, I saw there was already an occupant in our row—a teenaged boy who looked a little green around the gills. After cramming our carry-ons in the overhead bin, I introduced Missy and myself to Junior, who was very polite and nervously explained that it was his first flight without his parents and he was feeling nauseous. He confessed sheepishly that he couldn't find his "sick sack" and was afraid he might need it. I pushed my selfish *I hope this doesn't cut into my naptime* thoughts aside and helped him calm down and gave him my "sick sack," then got Missy situated watching a Dora movie on my iPad with her pink headphones and a bag of Cheez-Its.

We'd already taxied down the runway and were taking off by the time I leaned back into my seat and closed my eyes. After only a minute or two, I thought, *This is weird, but I just* know *somebody's staring at me . . . I can* feel *it.* So I opened my eyes and, sure enough, the flight attendant in the jump seat facing me—who was only about six or seven feet away—was staring directly at me, smiling. I smiled back warily, thinking she was being a tad intrusive, but then she gestured down at Missy and smiled wider. The noise of the jet engines was too loud to converse with words, but I knew instantly what she was saying because of a miraculous phenomenon called *estro-phonics,* the unique language wherein women are able to communicate solely through hand gestures, shoulder shrugs, and exaggerated facial expressions—especially in the brow region.

Wordlessly she mimed, "Your little girl is *so* cute!" And I mimed back, "I know, thank you!" Now, in print, the phrase, "I know," probably comes across as braggadocious. But trust me, it's much softer when mimed. I have very little pride attached to acknowledging my punkin's beauty because I didn't have any-thing to do with her DNA. Plus, at least once a month in Target or at the grocery store some yahoo stops us and squeals, "Ma'am, your *granddaughter* is so cute!" so that keeps my pride in check.

After our sweet, wordless exchange about how darling Missy is, I nodded, "Good-bye now," and leaned back into my seat a second time for my much-anticipated nap. But no sooner had I closed my eyes than I thought, *Now it sounds like that flight attendant is laughing.* I wasn't sure because I was wearing noise-cancelation headphones (although I bought a cheap pair so noise leaks in mine). So I opened my eyes again to check, and sure enough, she was still looking at us, only now she was laughing. My first thought was, *This chick needs to get a hobby.* But then I noticed she was gesturing at Missy again as if to say, "Look!"

Before I go any further in this story, I need to make a confession of my own. I'm at the age and stage of life that it behooves me to wear very constrictive undergarments—to keep my body parts in vaguely the same region God intended them to be. And because of the tensile strength of my unmentionables, sometimes I can't feel my extremities. Okay, back to the story.

I followed my new friend's mimed directive and looked down at Missy, only to discover her absentmindedly rubbing my chest (which I hadn't felt because of the above qualification) with her left hand while still engrossed in her educational cartoon. Then I noticed her mouth was moving, but I couldn't hear what she was saying—nor could she!—because we were both wearing headphones. So I pulled back my right earmuff and leaned down just in time to hear my baby bellow, "MAMA, I JUST LUB YOUR BREASTS! I LUB YOUR BREASTS!" At which point I realized that it wasn't just the flight attendant who was laughing at my child's wildly enthusiastic proclamation, but the rest of the passengers in the rear of the plane were roaring with delight too. Well, everybody except the teenaged boy sitting beside Missy. He was crimson and slowly sliding lower and lower into his seat!

We laugh *a lot* in our little family. Sometimes it's a hearty guffaw like when Missy groped me in public. But sometimes it's a less boisterous giggle like the one I had while driving home from an event in Memphis. Missy had informed me she needed to stop to go to the restroom twice with increasing intensity, and both times I'd explained that I'd stop just as soon as we got to an exit with a decent gas station or fast-food restaurant. After driving in silence a few more minutes, she said with noticeable angst, "Mama, I need to go potty so bad my bottom is *worried*!"

Given our proclivity for chuckling, I was thrilled to learn recently that laughter has legitimate health benefits. In fact, preliminary studies show that laughter normalizes levels of the stress hormone cortisol, which boosts immune function and reduces inflammation.[1] This is a huge win-win for us since Missy is HIV-positive, and I'm often in a fluffy season and need to drop a few pounds. Of course, that's not a guarantee I'll still be able to fit into my jeans if I laugh while inhaling chips and queso, but I'm sure willing to give it a go!

What *is* a guarantee about laughter is that *it was created by God:*

> For everything was created by him, in heaven and on earth, the visible and the invisible, whether thrones or dominions, or rulers or authorities—all things have been created through him and for him. (Col. 1:16)

It's a characteristic of God:

The one enthroned in heaven laughs . . . (Ps. 2:4a)

And it's a gift from God:

He will yet fill your mouth with laughter, and your lips with shouts of joy. (Job 8:21 NRSV)

It's also a tangible expression of happiness because it's how old and overjoyed Sarah responded when she went from wearing Depends to buying Pampers for her and Abraham's miracle baby, Isaac:

Sarah said, "God has brought me laughter, and everyone who hears about this will laugh with me." (Gen. 21:6 NIV)

As well as how the Israelites joyfully expressed their gratitude for God's mercy:

When the LORD brought the prisoners back to Jerusalem,
    it seemed as if we were dreaming.
Then we were filled with laughter,
    and we sang happy songs.
Then the other nations said,
    "The LORD has done great things for them."
The LORD has done great things for us,
    and we are very glad. (Ps. 126:1–3 NCV)

And it's how the wise woman from Proverbs 31 faces the future because she knows it's in God's hands:

She is clothed with strength and dignity, and she laughs without fear of the future. (Prov. 31:25 NLT)

According to Scripture, God's people laugh when they're happy. It's just what we do.

———

Now before you read any further, I'd like to go on record by saying that I was raised in the Baptist tradition. Well, technically, Mama was a Baptist, but Dad Harper segued from Nazarene to Pentecostal, so I guess it's more accurate to say I was raised in the Bapticostal tradition. The bottom line is I grew up believing—with no small influence from Mom and church leaders—that dancing was a big ole whopper of a sin, right up there with cussing, beer drinking, and card playing. I was convinced that much like in the movie *Footloose* (which my mom derided as "trashy"), if I ever gave into boogie fever, our pastor would excoriate me in front of the whole town, riots would ensue, and quite possibly our front lawn would be vandalized with discarded disco balls.

So it came as quite a shock to discover dancing is allowed in God's family. Like laughter, dancing is a harbinger of His amazing gift of happiness. I know, shut the front door, right? I mean, most of us are familiar with the no-holds-barred boogie fever King David expressed when the Israelites finally got to bring the ark of the covenant back home where it belonged in Jerusalem:

And David danced before the LORD with all his might. And David was wearing a linen ephod. So David and all the house of Israel brought up the ark of the LORD with shouting and with the sound of the horn. (2 Sam. 6:14–15 ESV) [The English Standard Version is as close to a word-for-word translation of the original texts as possible. Therefore, the word *danced* in verse 14 is the exact word used in the original language.]

But it's easy to chalk that incident up as situational. That was basically the Old Testament version of winning the Super Bowl or the World Cup, so it's understandable the king would go a little crazy. However, are you aware that God doesn't just *allow* His people to dance? He actually *commands* us to dance. Yup. Here's the decree, right smack-dab in the middle of the Bible, y'all:

Hallelujah! Praise God in his sanctuary. Praise him in his mighty expanse. Praise him for his powerful acts; praise him for his abundant greatness. Praise him with trumpet blast; praise him with harp and lyre. Praise him with tambourine and *dance*; praise him with strings and flute. Praise him with resounding cymbals; praise him with clashing symbols. Let everything that breathes praise the LORD! (Ps. 150, emphasis mine)

In chapter 1 we established that the Psalter literally *begins* with the word *happy* and promises genuine joy for those who walk in God's ways:

Happy are those who don't listen to the wicked, who don't go where sinners go, who don't do what evil people do. They love the LORD's teachings, and they think about those teachings day and night. They are strong, like a tree planted by a river. The tree produces fruit in season, and its leaves don't die. Everything they do will succeed. (Ps. 1:1–3 NCV, emphasis mine)

So it seems especially fitting that the finale directs us to dance because of the joy we feel as a result of His faithfulness:

Praise him with tambourines and *dancing* . . . (Ps. 150:4 NCV, emphasis mine)

In light of all the themes the ancient hymnwriters explore in these 150 psalms/songs—feasts and famines, joy and sorrow, life and death, friends and foes—God's loving presence is unmistakable throughout. Regardless of how difficult and disheartening life got, these Old Testament musicians knew God was sovereign and full of compassion. That ultimately, everything really would work out for their good and His glory, as another sacred journalist penned on parchment centuries later in Romans 8:28.

And let's not forget, the psalmists were *looking forward* to Jesus. They believed God's promises but didn't get to experience a flesh-and-blood Messiah. However, we live on the "Christmas and Easter really happened" side of progressive revelation. We *know* Jesus came to this earth in the form of an incarnate baby born in Bethlehem and was laid in a cattle trough. We *know* He lived a perfect, sinless life. We *know* after thirty-plus years He will-ingly walked up a hill and stretched out His arms to be nailed to a tree in order for His blood to justify our sin. We can hold New Testament historical accounts of Jesus' crucifixion and resurrec-tion in our own hands. Therefore, we have an *even greater* reason to dance than the psalmists and their contemporaries, don't we?

Alas, my gut tells me some of you dear readers are still resistant to wiggle while you worship or laugh with abandon lest you appear undignified, immature, or, worse still, *unspiritual*. Or perhaps you think your personality type doesn't lend itself to overt expressions of happy. I had a woman sincerely inform me recently that she was both a Presbyterian and an introvert, and therefore "guffaw" and "boogie" were not in her natural repertoire. It was such a privilege to get to sit down with her and explain the *supernatural* aspect of laughter and dance—that true, biblical happiness doesn't have a personality type!

—

A friend of mine, Sarah, who's a vocational worship leader, recently shared something that happened while she was lead-ing worship at a multidenominational women's conference. She described how the right side of the convention center was filled with more conservative Christ-followers who sang along melodi-cally with subdued clapping as she led worship, whereas the left side was populated with women from traditionally charismatic denominations who were much more demonstrative. They clapped really loudly, swayed to the rhythm of the music, and sometimes even shouted phrases like "Glory to God!" or "Thank You, Jesus!" between songs.

During the lunch break, a few women from the right cornered Sarah and said they felt like the other side's effusiveness was highly inappropriate. (Not unlike when King David's wife, Michal, turned her nose up in extreme disdain over his public display of pure joy: "Then it happened as the ark of the LORD came into the city of David that Michal the daughter of Saul looked out of the window and saw King David leaping and dancing before the LORD; and she despised him in her heart" [2 Sam. 6:16 NASB]). They complained that such noisy and overt expressions of praise were distracting and made them feel uncomfortable. Then they primly asked her to encourage the girls on the left to tone it down a bit. So prior to the next worship session, my friend reluctantly approached the leader of the loud girls and explained the situation. The leader's face fell with disappointment, but she graciously agreed to ask "her side" to temper their zeal. Then she said wistfully if only the others knew what God had rescued them from—drug addiction, physical abuse, paralyzing shame from abortions, etc.—perhaps they'd be more tolerant of their enthusiasm.

Sarah's heart broke during the first song of the next set because those precious women who'd been so full of life now seemed deflated. Their earnest enthusiasm was replaced with undeserved disgrace. Propriety had trumped passion. So she stopped strumming her guitar and started speaking her mind. She expressed regret for asking anyone to rein in her ardor for Jesus. She lamented the way Christians tend to value decorum more than divine grace. Then she repeated the leader's lament about how if the others knew from what the "boisterous brigade" had been mercifully and miraculously saved, they might be a little less judgmental. By the time my friend stopped teaching and started singing again, she said even some of the stiff chicks were attempting to boogie with the beat!

Sarah's experience reminds me of the woman who washed Jesus' feet with her tears, dried them with her hair, and then anointed them with expensive perfume (Luke 7:36–50). Religious people misinterpreted her behavior as being too demonstrative as well. But Jesus justified her extravagance when He proclaimed, "She was forgiven many, many sins, and so she is very, very grateful" (Luke 7:47 MSG).

The jubilant dance described in Psalm 150 isn't just for Pentecostals or extroverts or folks with rhythm. It's a biblical template for joyful believers to express how very, very grateful we are for God's mercy and forgiveness! Mind you, our boogying doesn't have to take place in public. Some of the happiest, and I daresay *holiest*, dances I've done are in the privacy of our own home twirling with Missy while Kari Jobe or Chris Tomlin lead us in worship as loud as our stereo can amplify their tunes.

———

Recently, I had my own encounter that served as a sort of exclamation point on this subject of happy dancing. I was speaking at a Christian retreat for people who'd struggled with alcohol abuse, drug addiction, serial adultery, and just about every other colorful sin you can imagine, which actually made for a very refreshing experience because recovering addicts tend to be candid about their mistakes and their desperate need for God's mercy. While personally I've never dealt with substance abuse, I did spend a big chunk of my life addicted to carbohydrates, abusive men, and other people's approval, so I couldn't help but think, *These are my people!* from the moment the event started.

And I couldn't stop watching one woman in the front row at the beginning of the first session because she danced during every single song. Her clothes were humble, her long hair was streaked with gray, but her upturned face was radiant. She seemed totally unaware—or at least unconcerned—that anyone might be watching her while she swayed and dipped and spun. I thought, *I bet she's got one of those amazing redemption stories like those women who danced at Sarah's conference.*

So I was delighted when I walked into the church before the conference began the next morning and found her sitting up front by herself. After I introduced myself, I told her how much I appreciated her pure, un-self-conscious worship the previous night. She seemed a little embarrassed, but mostly pleased, and then began enthusing how Jesus had restored her from a horrible childhood of poverty and physical abuse and redeemed her from a nightmarish adult life of drugs, booze, and bad men. I'll never forget how her eyes sparkled when she declared in a firm, gravelly Southern accent, "Miss Lisa, I cain't help *but* dance!"

As I fall more in love with Jesus, I pray my expression of joyful worship will be as pure and exuberant as hers. With my daughter as a tutor, I think I'm headed in the right direction!

Missy now loves to sing a song I learned when I was a little girl, and it starts like this:

If you're happy and you know it . . .

You remember it too, don't you? I think for the sake of the sacrament of happy it would be more than appropriate for us to tweak the lyrics of that familiar tune and sing it this way until laughing and dancing *are* part of our natural repertoire:

If you're happy and you know it, laugh and dance.
If you're happy and you know it, laugh and dance.
If you're happy and you know it, then you should surely show it.
If you're happy and you know it, laugh and dance!

The Practical Pursuit of Happiness

1. Do you tend to be a loud laugher or more of a quiet chuckler?

_____

_____

_____

2. When is the last time you laughed so hard you cried (or if you're like me, perhaps your bladder decided to join in the fun!)?

_____

_____

_____

3. Reread Psalm 126:1–3. When—if ever—have you belly laughed in a spiritual setting?

_____

_____

_____

4. Have you ever been encouraged to "temper your zeal" in a spiritual setting? If so, how did it make you feel?

_____

_____

_____

5. When and how does propriety tend to trump passion in your relationship with Jesus?

_____

_____

_____

6. What chapter of your redemption story has the most potential to shock your church/small group friends?

_____

_____

_____

7. Read Luke 7:36–50. In what ways can you identity with the woman who was so undone by Christ's compassion that she washed His feet with her tears and dried them with her hair?

_____

_____

_____

Is Happiness the Absence of Sadness?

While other worldviews lead us to sit in the midst of life's joys, foreseeing the coming sorrows, Christianity empowers its people to sit in the midst of this world's sorrows, tasting the coming joy.[1]
Tim Keller

A DEAR FRIEND OF MINE LOST HER THIRTEEN-YEAR-OLD son in a tragic misadventure in their backyard recently. He was a bright-eyed, fair-haired, mischievous, Huck Finn type of kid—not yet fully grown. He was more like a man-child filled with promise of who he was to become. Those of us who gathered at their home in the hours and days following his death were soft-spoken and red-eyed, deeply jarred by the terrible sadness of it all and deeply concerned about our friends and their younger son who lost his very best friend in the whole world.

A few days after the tragedy, another friend and I were standing quietly in their driveway—we'd done what we could for the moment and were just waiting to see if another task presented itself—when she asked softly, "This shouldn't have happened. It's just so horrible. How will they ever be happy again?" It was more of a compassionate observation than a question, and I wasn't about to sully her empathy by saying anything out loud, but the gist of her question has reverberated in my heart since: "Is it possible to be happy after horrible things happen to us or to those we love?"

Children shouldn't die before their parents. They shouldn't be born with devastating birth defects or cancer or cerebral palsy. Families in minivans shouldn't be killed by drunk drivers. Moms and dads shouldn't stop loving each other and spew hatred and discord during their divorce process. Friends shouldn't become enemies. Sex shouldn't be abusive. Earthquakes shouldn't wipe out entire villages. Pastors shouldn't have affairs and leave the whole congregation feeling stunned and betrayed. There should be no such thing as a suicide bomber.

None of this seems remotely congruent with the idea of real, recurrent happiness, does it? Yet all we have to do is turn on a television, scroll through social media, or poll the people in our neighborhood for proof that it happens Every. Single. Day. Before you finish reading this sentence, someone else, somewhere else in the world—or possibly even one of your dear friends—will experience something tragic. Their personal version of: *this shouldn't have happened.* Frankly, dear reader, I'm sure something that "shouldn't have" *has* happened to you. Because we live in a broken world. One that was marred from the start when Eve got deceived by a slithery liar and stepped out of the perfect existence God created for us in Eden. After that evil snake named satan (I refuse to capitalize his name, and thankfully my publisher agrees wholeheartedly with this minor grammatical mutiny) hissed his first lie, nobody had a chance of getting out of here unscathed.

Therefore, since life as we know it is inherently flawed and culture is a poor conduit of true, soul-satisfying happiness, where does that leave us? Should we despondently hurl every book and DVD that includes the concept of happy into a raging bonfire? Should we forgo sitcoms with laugh tracks and only watch nature shows where the cheetah actually catches the limping baby antelope? Is it possible for happiness, sadness, and even "badness" to coexist? And if so, how do we orient our lives to be authentically joyful while not ignoring or becoming immune to the calamity and chaos around us and sometimes in us?

The key to hanging on to our happy—our deep sense of fulfillment, contentment, and delight—when horrible things happen is to recognize this:

Real, God-imbued happiness is not the absence of sadness or badness. Rather, it is hanging on to the truth of His sovereign goodness regardless of what's going on within or around us.

The Bible makes it abundantly clear that happy and sad are *not* mutually exclusive. In fact, these two passages from Proverbs and Lamentations, as well as several others, imply they're more like two sides of the same coin:

Even in laughter the heart may ache, and the end of joy may be grief. (Prov. 14:13 ESV)

My soul is bereft of peace; I have forgotten what happiness is; so I say, "My endurance has perished; so has my hope from the LORD." Remember my affliction and my wanderings, the wormwood and the gall! My soul continually remembers it and is bowed down within me. But this I call to mind, and therefore I have hope:

The steadfast love of the LORD never ceases; his mercies never come to an end; they are new every morning; great is your faithfulness. (Lam. 3:17–23 ESV)

To forget what happiness is *and* remember the hope we have because of God's steadfast love . . . that's the poignant paradox of Christianity. Delight and despair absolutely coexist. They ebb and flow like the tides. Grief may surge while happy hangs back a bit, and vice versa. However, in Christ, each wholly exists in the heart of mankind. Circumstances may prompt one to rise to the occasion and eclipse the other for a while. And our personality bent may compel us to manifest one more readily than the other. But the proverbial bucket that dips into the well of our souls has the potential to scoop up both genuine joy and profound sorrow.

Furthermore, while this divine dichotomy may sound like an emotional Rubik's Cube that's nearly impossible to live out, there are actually quite a few saints who model it beautifully. Take Hannah, for instance. When we're initially introduced to her in the Old Testament book of 1 Samuel, her story seems anything but happy:

> There was a man named Elkanah who lived in Ramah in the region of Zuph in the hill country of Ephraim. He was the son of Jeroham, son of Elihu, son of Tohu, son of Zuph, of Ephraim. Elkanah had two wives, Hannah and Peninnah. Peninnah had children, but Hannah did not. Each year Elkanah would travel to Shiloh to worship and sacrifice to the LORD of Heaven's Armies at the Tabernacle. The priests of the LORD at that time were the two sons of Eli—Hophni and Phinehas. On the days Elkanah presented his sacrifice, he would give portions of the meat to Peninnah and each of her children. And though he loved Hannah, he would give her only one choice portion because the LORD had given her no children. So Peninnah would taunt Hannah and make fun of her because the LORD had kept her from having

children. Year after year it was the same—Peninnah would taunt Hannah as they went to the Tabernacle. Each time, Hannah would be reduced to tears and would not even eat. (1 Sam. 1:1–7 NLT)

Good night, no wonder she was so sad she couldn't eat. Not only did she have to struggle with infertility, but she also had to deal with a super obnoxious sister-wife who took every opportunity to rub her "Fertile-Myrtle" status in Hannah's face. Ugh. Can you imagine their conversation on the way to Costco in the family minivan?

Peninnah/Taunter (bellows in a high, nasally voice while wearing a self-satisfied smirk and rubbing her ginormous belly): *OMG, Hannah! Here I am pregnant with triplets and 'Kanah and I already have these SIX rugrats.* (At which point she rolls her eyes and gestures toward the rowdy, roughhousing brood behind her. None of whom are buckled in, and several are hanging out the van windows hurling detritus at other vehicles.)

Hannah/Tauntee (mumbles sadly, while driving with one hand and trying to pull a piece of chewing gum—flung by one of Peninnah's hooligans—out of her hair with the other): *Mmmm-hmmm.*

Peninnah/Taunter (who's now taken off her shoes, put both feet on the dashboard, and started clipping her chipped red toenails with a clipper she found while digging through Hannah's neatly organized purse without asking): *I mean, all 'Kanah has to do is smile at me and POW—there's another bun in my oven! I mean, when it comes to gettin' knocked up I'm a dad-gum Olympic champion! But you've been trying to have a kid with him for what—ten years now?—and still no baby! Girl, I have to tell you, when it comes to gettin' pregnant, you're like a nun in Vegas . . . it's just not your scene, Little Miss Hannah-Banana!* (After which Peninnah slaps Hannah's thigh and begins to cackle derisively, which quickly dissolves into a coughing fit due to Peninnah's two-pack-a-day smoking habit.)

Good night, that's a tough row to hoe right there.

Fortunately, despite his proclivity for polygamy, her husband was sensitive to Hannah's heartache and publically favored her over prideful Peninnah (1 Sam. 1:5, 8). But she was still so disheartened by her situation that she poured her heart out so dramatically at the altar. The priest on duty thought she'd had one too many glasses of wine before coming to church:

> Once after a sacrificial meal at Shiloh, Hannah got up and went to pray. Eli the priest was sitting at his customary place beside the entrance of the Tabernacle. Hannah was in deep anguish, crying bitterly as she prayed to the LORD. And she made this vow: "O LORD of Heaven's Armies, if you will look upon my sorrow and answer my prayer and give me a son, then I will give him back to you. He will be yours for his entire lifetime, and as a sign that he has been dedicated to the LORD, his hair will never be cut." As she was praying to the LORD, Eli watched her. Seeing her lips moving but hearing no sound, he thought

she had been drinking. "Must you come here drunk?" he demanded. "Throw away your wine!" "Oh no, sir!" she replied. "I haven't been drinking wine or anything stronger. But I am very discouraged, and I was pouring out my heart to the LORD. Don't think I am a wicked woman! For I have been praying out of *great* anguish and sorrow." (1 Sam. 1:9–16 NLT, emphasis mine)

I'm so glad this passage clarifies that Hannah was emoting *greatly* in God's house. That she wasn't stuffing her feelings to appear more appropriate or pious. Because I tend to emote greatly as well, and I believe one of the biggest fallacies woven into many communities of faith is that the closer we get to Jesus the more we need to keep a lid on it. Or that we shouldn't guffaw with gusto lest we might somehow distract God and throw Him off His game. Or better yet, we shouldn't weep uncontrollably because we could sully His reputation as the perfect Comforter. Thankfully, Hannah gives us a biblical model of how to carry our deepest sorrow and desperation to the Lord even when those around us completely misunderstand our grief.

To say I was an emoting church kid would be an understatement. I can't even begin to tell you how many congregational stink eyes I received in those early years. By the time I was five or six years old, I knew I was likely destined to stand facing the corner in God's house in heaven. The adults around me had made it crystal clear that He preferred quiet kids who didn't ask too many questions in Sunday school, bellow when they sang in the children's choir, or reenact scenes from Tarzan and Jane with the pastor's son using the balcony balustrades as vines. I learned the hard way that being "demonstrative" was right up there with big, brow-raising no-no's like drinking and dancing and tattoos.

Sadly, my distorted youthful vision of God as some uni-browed grump who walks around with a giant mute button took decades to correct. This perception resulted in the secret, stubborn belief that I wasn't good enough for God throughout childhood, adolescence, and early adulthood. It also made me a magnet for scoffing (Remember the happy hijackers in Psalm 1?), Peninnah-kind-of-folks who enjoy nothing more than pushing others into shame pits.

Case in point—my old boyfriend who moonlighted as a buzzkiller. To be fair, he was an intellectual genius with an Ivy League PhD. I think his brain got so big pondering things like Einstein's theory of relativity that his heart barely had room to breathe, much less engage in things like interpersonal relation-ships. Plus, I'm sure he's a different, more sensitive man now. At least I hope he is for his wife's sake!

Anyway, early on in our friendship, he informed me that I talked too much. I know, *shocker*. But it wasn't the obvious information that bothered me—I mean, I've been aware of my windbag proclivity for as long as I can remember—but rather the demeaning way he attempted to decrease my word count. Whenever we were on the phone and I got a little too long-winded or descriptive for his taste, he would depress one of the numeral buttons on his phone for about ten seconds, which resulted in an elongated, shrill *BEEP* on my end.

The first couple of times he beeped me I thought it was by accident. Then, when the tones increased in volume and consistency, I thought perhaps he'd fallen asleep while we were chatting, which—given all the mental energy he exerted both at work and solving complicated mathematical problems in his head "for fun" during his free time—made perfect sense to me. I mused affectionately, *Poor fella, he's probably so exhausted he doesn't realize his strong, masculine jawline is jutting into his key pad causing me audible trauma.*

It wasn't until he informed me matter-of-factly that I was a "controlled" variable in a little experiment he was conducting that I realized he'd been zapping me on purpose. He explained—rather verbosely, I might add!—that based on Pavlovian research (Remember the slobbering dog/dinner bell experiment we studied in high school?), he formed a hypothesis that involved attaching a tangible negative consequence to my loquaciousness to see if it would pare down my verbal paragraphs. Completely oblivious to what I'm sure was an expression of shame and humiliation on my face, he blithely concluded that the zapping had resulted in a satisfactory editing effect and I was, in fact, talking less.

Now you're probably thinking, *I bet she kicked his sorry tail to the curb!* But I didn't. At least not for several months. Instead, I developed a stammering habit and assumed his oppressive behavior was what spiritual maturity and leadership looked like because, after all, God Himself favors less chatty, less emotive chicks, right? Wrong! So. Very. Wrong.

Unless you work in a theater, symphony hall, surgical suite, or library, I encourage you to graciously scoot shushing scoffers to the edge of your life where they're mostly out of earshot. Unless you're a writer by trade, you probably don't need an editor. At least not one who's energetic about pointing out your flaws! We all need friends who speak the truth in love (Proverbs 27:6 says the wounds of a friend are better than the kiss of an enemy), but we don't need mean-spirited buzzkillers who attempt to hijack our happy because they don't have enough fulfillment, contentment, and delight of their own.

———

Now back to Hannah. In the space of one single chapter, she goes from begging God for a child with so much passionate grief that the priest observing her assumed she was tipsy to happily giving birth to a boy named Samuel—which literally means "The Lord Heard"—who went on to become one of the greatest spiritual leaders in biblical history. The seemingly polar contrast of her going from profoundly sad to wildly celebratory could've landed a less stable woman in a padded cell. I mean, that's quite a stretch, isn't it? But Hannah's emotional flexibility lies in her deep faith in God's absolute, unwavering goodness. Whether she was standing on a proverbial mountaintop of happiness or trudging through a valley of sorrow, Hannah knew that God had her back.

Just listen to the lyrics of the tune she sang after dropping off her desperately-longed-for-little-boy Samuel at the temple to be raised and mentored in the art of priesthood by Eli, the very same guy who initially judged her to be inebriated at the altar. That's right, after Samuel was "weaned" or stopped breast-feeding—which, in her era of ancient history, meant he was around the age of three or four—Hannah selflessly enrolled him in holy boarding school. She basically gave him right back to God, knowing full well that meant she would only get to see her precious son on rare weekend visits and maybe for a week or two during the summer. Yet her sacrificial song is filled with exultant joy:

> My heart rejoices in the LORD;
>> my horn is lifted up by the LORD.
> My mouth boasts over my enemies,
>> because I rejoice in your salvation.
> There is no one holy like the LORD.
> There is no one besides you!
> And there is no rock like our God.
> Do not boast so proudly,
>> or let arrogant words come out of your mouth,
>> for the LORD is a God of knowledge,
>> and actions are weighed by him.
> The bows of the warriors are broken,
>> but the feeble are clothed with strength.

Those who are full hire themselves out for food,
  but those who are starving hunger no more.
The woman who is childless gives birth to seven,
  but the woman with many sons pines away.
The LORD brings death and gives life;
  he sends some down to Sheol, and he raises others
  up.
The LORD brings poverty and gives wealth;
  he humbles and he exalts.
He raises the poor from the dust
  and lifts the needy from the trash heap.
He seats them with noblemen
  and gives them a throne of honor.
For the foundations of the earth are the LORD's;
  he has set the world on them.
He guards the steps of his faithful ones,
  but the wicked perish in darkness,
  for a person does not prevail by his own strength.
Those who oppose the LORD will be shattered;
  he will thunder in the heavens against them.
The LORD will judge the ends of the earth.
He will give power to his king;
  he will lift up the horn of his anointed.
(1 Sam. 2:1–10)

Theological scholars often draw parallels between Hannah's hymn of praise and Mary's Magnificat, the song the young virgin sang after finding out she'd been chosen to give birth to Jesus:

And Mary said:

My soul praises the greatness of the Lord, and my spirit rejoices in God my Savior, because he has looked with favor on the humble condition of his servant.

Surely, from now on all generations will call me blessed, because the Mighty One has done great things for me, and his name is holy.

His mercy is from generation to generation on those who fear him.

He has done a mighty deed with his arm; he has scattered the proud because of the thoughts of their hearts; he has toppled the mighty from their thrones and exalted the lowly.

He has satisfied the hungry with good things and sent the rich away empty.

He has helped his servant Israel, remembering his mercy to Abraham and his descendants forever, just as he spoke to our ancestors. (Luke 1:46–55, emphasis mine)

Both songs depict God elevating the humble and opposing the proud. Both demonstrate overt and unmuted—albeit unlikely, given their current circumstances—expressions of praise and gratitude. And if I may be so bold, I believe both also illustrate the posture of biblical happiness: *clinging* to the steadfast, sovereign mercy and kindness of our Redeemer regardless of what's going on around us. It is trusting that despite our inevitable disappointments and even our deepest distress, God's plan for us will ultimately prove itself to be immeasurably better than our best dream.

Genuine, God-given happiness is *not* the absence of sadness . . . it is the overriding presence of His sovereign mercy. The firm belief that *He is good* and *He does good* no matter what our current circumstances are.

If you are currently in a season punctuated with profound sadness and sorrow, I hope Hannah's story encouraged you that the veil is thinner there. If you'll follow her lead and allow God to cup your face in His perfectly loving hands and lift your head ever so slightly, you'll begin to notice an exquisite kind of luminescent grace that's only visible during the darkest nights of grief. I observed it recently in the home of my dear friend who's desperately missing her sweet son. A kind of delicate grace glimmered in the rows of Tupperware containers stacked neatly in her refrigerator, filled with home-cooked meals prepared by friends who are committed to help sustain her family throughout the grueling journey ahead. It was refracted in dozens of shimmering beams as her community sacrificed and postponed significant events in their own lives—vacations, taking a child to college, celebrating a birthday, work commitments—without hesitation in order to help her type the obituary for her "precious" seventh grader, take her younger son to a ballgame, or steam her dress for the funeral. The knowing reflection of shared anguish in her husband's gaze was more beautiful than the breathtaking lights of the aurora borealis I was once undone by while visiting Alaska.

It would be a trite and disgusting disregard of my friend's story to imply her future happiness will not include sadness, because the premature death of their beloved firstborn son has left behind an aroma of loss in the very fabric of their family life. They will always grieve his absence. But they *will* experience genuine happiness again too. They *will* experience contentment and fulfillment and even delight because the fragrance of God's abiding mercy will always prove itself stronger still than the most pungent loss. The notes of happy comingle with sad in the scent of God's people creating the loveliest perfume that others can't help but notice.

The Practical Pursuit of Happiness

1. What was your initial response to Tim Keller's quote at the beginning of this chapter?

_____

_____

_____

2. How have you experienced "sitting in the midst of this world's sorrows, tasting the coming joy" recently?

_____

_____

_____

3. When you first put your hope in Jesus, did you assume He'd somehow make your life easier, if not completely painless? If so, how long did it take you to figure out otherwise?

_____

_____

_____

4. Read Matthew 5:45. How would you explain this biblical truism to a child?

_____

_____

_____

5. How have the "tides" of happy and sad ebbed and flowed in your life this season?

_____

_____

_____

6. Would you describe yourself as being emotionally flexible? If so, how has your relationship with Jesus made you more resilient with life's difficulties and disappointments?

---

7. Read Psalm 56:8. Based on the last year of your life, is God's "concern carafe" for you full, half-full, or almost empty?

CHAPTER SEVEN

What about When Happy Takes a Hike?

*There is no automatic joy. Christ is not a
happiness capsule; he is the way to the Father.
But the way to the Father is not a carnival
ride in which we sit and do nothing while we
are whisked through various sensations.*
Calvin Miller

A FEW YEARS AGO I WAS CARPOOLING TO A SOCIAL EVENT
with a few friends and acquaintances and one of them kept com-
plaining the entire trip. I didn't know her well but had heard she
was a bit of a Negative Nancy, so after a while I just joined in

with the other girls and mumbled noncommittal "mmm hmmms" to her whiny, glass-is-half-empty declarations.

> *If the traffic doesn't thin out, we're going to be late.* Mmm. Hmmm.
>
> *If that car in the next lane gets any closer, he's going to ram us.* Mmm. Hmmm.
>
> *If it gets any hotter, I'm going to break out in a heat rash.* Mmm. Hmmm.
>
> *If they don't have lactose-free options tonight, I'm either going to starve or have terrible gas.* Mmm. Hmmm.
>
> *If the stock market gets any more volatile, there will be a global financial crisis.* Mmm. Hmmm.
>
> *If she swerves again, I'm going to throw up.*

At which point I couldn't take her Eeyore-isms anymore so I said something along the lines of, "Mind over matter usually works for me, so maybe if you don't think about being carsick you won't feel nauseous." I even said it with a smile. But I may as well have said, "You are a horrible creature with a really big bottom and we're all wishing we could pull over and dump you out on the side of the interstate right about now because you're getting on our collective last nerve." Because she gave me a withering look and then retorted snidely, "Well, excuse me, Lisa, but I wasn't born all *happy-go-lucky* like you." I so wanted to snap back, "Baby, my happy has *nothing* to do with luck. I've worked my tail off for my joy—my happy didn't just *happen!*" However, I didn't want to risk being punched in the nose so I just thought it very quietly to myself.

The truth is, no one's happiness is based on luck if his or her joy is genuine. Happy is not the result of happenstance. It's not a fluke, an accident, or largely dependent on our circumstances. As a matter of fact, scientific research reveals that *only* 10 percent of our happiness is connected to our circumstances, 50 percent is linked to genetic factors and temperament, and the other 40 percent is entirely within our control because it's determined by our choices, thoughts, and behavior.[1] *Did you get that?* ALMOST HALF OF THE DETERMINING FACTORS FOR HAPPINESS ARE REGULATED BY US! Good night, y'all! That means even if your hair is chemically dependent, your metabolism has slowed to a crawl, your online dating algorithms are all whacked out and you keep being matched with men who are unemployed and live in their mother's basement (I'm just going out on a limb here and speaking metaphorically, of course), you can still *choose* to be joyful! Our thought life doesn't have to be the boss of us!

Frankly, if we've put our hope in Jesus Christ, our thought life is under the authority of the Holy Spirit. That doesn't mean every single thing that sails through that space between our ears will be sacred, but we don't have to be controlled by pessimism, cynicism, or fear. As Martin Luther brilliantly observed, "You can't stop the birds from flying over your head, but you can keep them from making a nest in your hair."

Of course, it's natural for all of us to go through seasons when we lose our spiritual groove and our happiness wanes. I'm sure that, like me, you have experienced days or weeks or years when it seemed like everything was going wrong and your soul was drooping as a result. Maybe you've slogged through difficulties like a catastrophic illness, the death of a loved one, a divorce, or bills that added up to more than the balance in your bank account. Or maybe your heart just feels flattened by the heartbreaking humanitarian crises we've witnessed around the globe in our lifetime.

No matter how the details of your story differ from mine, I'll bet you can easily recall a time when you felt overwhelmed with disappointment, sorrow, or even hopelessness. When it seemed your prayers for relief weren't getting past the ceiling. When you ran out of joy juice while hiking up steep emotional hills.

When I really began dealing with—and feeling—the trauma of my childhood, I was inspired to be more candid about those struggles and drop the happy "act" after reading how C. S. Lewis struggled with debilitating sadness and questioned God's goodness after losing his wife, Joy, to cancer. Then, as I continued to mature emotionally, I delved even further into the subject matter of how happiness is often woven with hardship. This led me to study the life of prolific pastor Charles Haddon Spurgeon, who battled with severe depression. Despite the fact that twenty-five thousand people bought copies of his sermons every week at the height of his ministry and he got to preach to ten million people before his death in 1892, Spurgeon still had days when he didn't want to get out of bed. Following one of his darkest moments he said, "There are dungeons beneath the castles of despair."[2] Now that I've passed the midpoint of my life, I've come to the firm belief that no one gets out of life without at least a little pain and anguish. Show me an adult who says they haven't, and they're either a fibber, mentally unbalanced or have amnesia.

I'm so grateful God gives us time and space and emotions capable of processing dark nights of the soul and that the gospel frees us from pretending we're joyful when we're not. But I'm even more glad that He gave us the mental faculties to ultimately recover our happy regardless of whether it was illegitimately hijacked or overshadowed by legitimate grief or suffering or pain. The following passages both affirm scientific research and the power our minds have to correct negative, destructive thought patterns:

> Do not conform to the pattern of this world, but be transformed by the renewing of your mind. Then you will be able to test and approve what God's will is—his good, pleasing and perfect will. (Rom. 12:2 NIV)

> "Who has known the mind of the Lord? Who has been able to teach him?" But we have the mind of Christ. (1 Cor. 2:16 NCV)

> For God has not given us a spirit of fear, but of power and of love and of a sound mind. (2 Tim. 1:7 NKJV)

In other words, with the Holy Spirit's help, you and I have the power to kick "stinkin' thinkin'" to the curb and recapture happiness!

———

I had lots of professional counseling, as well as peer counseling (with other adoptive parents), before bringing Missy home from Haiti, and one of the common rules of thumb was to be careful about overstimulation, especially while she was settling in. Like most newly adoptive parents, I was advised against taking her to large public events (like a college or professional football game), playing loud music, or even inviting more than a few people over to our home at one time while Missy was initially adapting to a completely foreign environment. A couple I know really well and trust almost implicitly with regards to parenting—they have four biological children and three adopted children, all of whom are kind, thriving, well-adjusted kids—warned me specifically about overwhelming Missy during our first Christmas together. They said too many gifts would probably overwhelm her and possibly even frighten her after the extreme scarcity she was used to in Haiti.

Remarkable restraint is the only way to describe me that Christmas, especially after I'd dreamed of a Clark Griswold kind of holiday with Missy. I had pictured lights everywhere, gifts piled up to the ceiling, and a massive fir tree flanked by fountains to accentuate the greenery from the moment I'd found out I was actually Going. To. Be. Her. Mama. I reluctantly scrapped all the neon and fountain plans and scaled way back on my shopping sprees, even though it about killed me to cancel the order for the pony with pink satin ribbons braided in her mane and tail. Of course, my friends and counselor were right. Missy was totally content with the small assortment of gifts I bought her, especially a battery-operated train that totally enchanted her even though it was the most basic model I could find. We spent most of that first Christmas together peacefully sprawled out in the living room, eating pizza or popcorn, and watching those three simple train cars go round and round and round. It was a lovely, very low-key affair.

However, this past Christmas I decided not to leave well enough alone. I'd waited to be a parent for decades, doggone it, which means I *earned* the right to stay up all night on Christmas Eve putting together giant, complex toys that came with a motor and/or instructions printed in Chinese! So I bought Missy a dozen or so ho-hum gifts like dolls and Legos, but was *especially* excited about her motorized mini Jeep and huge outdoor, competition-sized trampoline. And I'm happy to report—despite the multiple broken fingernails, bruises, and one wee gash over the eye I sustained while putting that vehicle and Olympian-in-training-worthy trampoline together—my child has neither had a mishap while driving nor sprained an arm while bouncing. Because even though I transformed into Santa on steroids for a few weeks there, I still had enough sense to install safeguards on those over-the-top toys. Her little Jeep won't go faster than a turtle-like five miles per hour, due to a governor I installed on the accelerator, and her jumbo-size trampoline is surrounded by an extra high net, double-bolted in place with ergonomic, heavily padded posts so it's nearly impossible for her to fall off. Sure, I got carried away, but I'm still not going to let my kid get *hurt*!

Plus, the precautions I installed to protect my little girl's body also contribute to protecting my mama heart. Just knowing an overweight tortoise could outrun her miniature Jeep and the heavy-duty trampoline net will keep her from accidentally catapulting to the hard ground below allow me to breathe easier and keep parental anxiety at bay.

Thankfully, there are several practical steps we can take to help safeguard our happy, too.

Safeguarding Our Happy

1. Frisk Your Thoughts

I know that may sound a tad sketchy, but it's actually based on a Bible verse:

> We demolish arguments and every pretension that sets itself up against the knowledge of God, and we take captive every thought to make it obedient to Christ. (2 Cor. 10:5 NIV)

I'd be rich if I had a nickel for every time my first boss in vocational ministry quoted that verse to me and then expounded in his strong Southern drawl, "Leeesa, ya' need to take yer thoughts CAPTIVE. Whenever a bad belief that doesn't honor Jeezus enters yer head, ya' just do exactly what the police do with violent felons—ya' secure it and frisk it!" The first time he used that analogy, I was flustered by the aggression it implied. Somehow slinging a thought against a wall sounded unspiritual, much less ladylike—unless you're into rollerderby. But the image stuck with me. And before long, I realized some of the lies the enemy had set loose in my mind like rats in a cheese shop *needed* to be hurled against bricks and checked for legitimacy. Because I'd let toxic untruths shoplift my joy for way too long.

That was thirty years ago, and I still employ his profound, albeit homespun, wisdom. Whenever I realize a potentially happy-hijacking thought has entered my mind like: *What if I can't afford health insurance in the future and then can't afford the exorbitant uninsured price for Missy's HIV meds?* I grab it as fast as I can by its scrawny shoulders and push it up against the bedrock wall of God's promises, causing flimsy, fear-pricking falsehoods to shatter against impervious truths like:

And my God will meet all your needs according to the riches of his glory in Christ Jesus. (Phil. 4:19 NIV)

Young lions lack food and go hungry, but those who seek the LORD will not lack any good thing. (Ps. 34:10)

For the LORD God is a sun and shield; the LORD bestows favor and honor. No good thing does he withhold from those who walk uprightly. (Ps. 84:11 ESV)

The LORD will not let the righteous go hungry, but he denies the wicked what they crave. (Prov. 10:3)

"Don't worry and say, 'What will we eat?' or 'What will we drink?' or 'What will we wear?' The people who don't know God keep trying to get these things, and your Father in heaven knows you need them." (Matt. 6:31–32 NCV)

"So if you sinful people know how to give good gifts to your children, how much more will your heavenly Father give good gifts to those who ask him." (Matt. 7:11 NLT)

"Consider the ravens, for they neither sow nor reap; they have no storeroom nor barn, and yet God feeds them; how much more valuable you are than the birds!" (Luke 12:24 NASB)

And God is able to make every grace overflow to you, so that in every way, always having everything you need, you may excel in every good work. (2 Cor. 9:8)

Suddenly the dragon's big fat fib about the possibility of my kid not getting the medicine she needs sounds pretty innocuous, doesn't it? I'm telling you, *frisking your thoughts* works!

2. Get Your Butt Out of Your Rut

This safeguard is another way to keep joy embezzlers out of our minds. We'll get to the spiritual, less colorful, application of this concept in chapter 9 when we consider how happiness can change the world. But for now I'm going with a lower common denominator and advising those of you who feel stuck in negativity to *move*. Literally. Go for a walk. Go fly a kite. Go to a movie. Go antiquing. Go grocery shopping. Go spelunking. Go to a puppet show. Go to a dog show. Go race go-carts. Just *do* something different from what you're currently doing!

This is one of the most interesting commands God gives Abraham, the father of our faith, near the beginning of biblical history:

> Now the LORD said to Abram, "Go from your country and your kindred and your father's house to the land that I will show you. And I will make of you a great nation, and I will bless you and make your name great, so that you will be a blessing. I will bless those who bless you, and him who dishonors you I will curse, and in you all the families of the earth shall be blessed." So Abram went, as the LORD had told him, and Lot went with him. (Gen. 12:1–4a ESV)

So before God ever clarified *how* He was going to bless Abram (whose name was soon changed to Abraham), a move was necessary. A change of direction had to take place for their covenant to be complete. Abraham had to leave everything that was familiar in order to be rewarded with something better than he could possibly imagine. Interesting how God's blessings often require us to budge from where we've gotten really comfortable, isn't it?

When I was in one of the deepest funks of my life, I confessed to my Christian counselor, Lynn, that I felt like a piece of bread in a pond filled with piranhas. (Because I didn't frisk that thought early on, it multiplied dramatically like one of those wee sponges that expands hugely when you add just few drops of water.) She'd been counseling me for months by then and had been very helpful, patient, and professional, but her response to my melodrama that day was more direct than usual. She looked into my eyes for a long moment and then asked sincerely with just a hint of reproach, "Well then, why don't you swim to the dock and get out of the pond?" That single question was worth years of therapy. Because for whatever reason, until she asked it, I hadn't considered that something as simple as changing my position could be so transformational. Sometimes even slightly shifting your position while looking out of the same window can dramatically change your view.

———

The first few years of Missy's life were incredibly difficult. She was born into abject poverty in a rural Haitian village to a single mother. Her mom grew increasingly sick and incapacitated from undiagnosed AIDS and eventually died when Missy was two and a half, unwittingly infecting her with HIV. The only person willing to take Missy in was her great-aunt Fifi, who was often sick with various physical ailments herself. And while Fifi adored her grandniece, she and Missy subsisted in a small shack and rarely had enough food to eat.

Unfortunately, because of Haiti's ever-changing adoption regulations, fifteen months into our adoption process, my little girl was effectively yanked from the safety of her beloved Fifi and the familiarity of their village and placed in a four-bedroom orphanage packed with sixty-plus other children and few adult caregivers who mostly kept their distance from her because they were afraid HIV could be transmitted through casual physical contact.

By the time I brought Missy home to Nashville when she was four and a half, whatever small happiness she'd known as a toddler had been replaced by wariness. Because I firmly believe in the biblical principle of reaping what you sow, I decided I was going to sow joy into my little girl. So I searched for opportunities to make her feel safe *and* happy from the very beginning. We went to play therapy where she processed the trauma she'd endured in Haiti *and* I made up crazy voices with puppets and storybook characters. I practiced meaningful touch and therapeutic massage *and* did silly, sliding pratfalls on our slick wood floors. Nighttime nurturing rituals were intentionally created *and* I sang some of her favorite lullabies loud and off-key (which is not much of a stretch for me). I danced in public almost everywhere we went to make her laugh. I did horrible imitations of John Travolta in the grocery store and Target aisles. I twirled in line at the bank and did lots of enthusiastic hand and shoulder gyrations to children's tunes belted through the car speakers while in traffic.

It took a long time for my daughter's heart to unfold and trust that I loved her and wasn't going to abandon her. But eventually her joy came bubbling to the surface like a dormant well that just needed extra priming. Now her belly laughs are every bit as loud and frequent as mine, and she dances multiple times a day with much more rhythm than me!

A few nights ago we were sitting in the backyard by the fire pit, enjoying how its warmth was taking the edge off of the chilly fall air, when our dog, Cookie, came barreling up through the brush from the bottom field. She skidded to a messy stop right in front of our Adirondack chairs and shook herself with canine glee, soaking us with stinky water from yet another swim in our neighbor's stagnant pond. Then she began licking Missy's face while thwacking me with her drippy, wildly wagging tail. I started laughing, but Missy—who can be quite the priss-pot—leaned back melodramatically (I don't know *where* she gets it from) and shrieked, "Ga-ross, Cookie! You are so *stanky*!"

After a sheepish sideways glance at me, Missy sighed loudly, scooted a few inches closer to our wet mutt, patted her gingerly on the top of the head, and said in a conciliatory tone, "But you are a veh-rie good dog and your stanky might keep da bugs from biting me!"

It was all I could do not to high-five toward heaven and cheer, "My job is done here, Lord!" because my precious peanut has already learned how to frisk her thoughts *and* get her wee butt out of a negative rut.

The Practical Pursuit of Happiness

1. Reread Martin Luther's quote about birds/nests/hair. What fowl has been fouling up your coiffure lately?

_____

_____

_____

2. How would you define a "sound" mind?

_____

_____

_____

3. What anxious and/or negative thoughts are the most common unwanted guests to traipse through your mind?

_____

_____

_____

4. Read Galatians 5:22–23. How does the size of your caboose fruit (self-control) compare with the rest of this list? (By the way, in the original Greek text, *fruit* is a singular, comprehensive term, which means when you put your hope in Jesus you get *all* of these characteristics. However, some of your spiritual fruit might be the size of a grape while others may be more along the lines of a watermelon!)

_____

_____

_____

5. Does your personality type lean more toward couch potato or Energizer Bunny?

_____

_____

_____

6. When has the Holy Spirit prompted you to move from a place of comfort (or rut of complacency) toward a totally new place that required radical trust on your part?

_____

_____

_____

7. What's one practical step you can take to more effectively frisk your thoughts and kick stinkin' thinkin' to the curb?

_____

_____

_____

CHAPTER
EIGHT

How Do We Cultivate Happy?

*Gratitude exclaims, very properly, "How
good of God to give me this."*
C. S. Lewis

ONE OF MY OLDEST AND HAPPIEST FRIENDS, EVA
Whittington Self, was paralyzed in a hit-and-run accident when
she was a senior in high school. Prior to the accident, she was a
vivacious cheerleader, basketball player, and good-natured, beautiful young woman. But then someone who was driving a car
way too fast during a spring snowstorm in North Carolina forced
Eva's car off the road, and she flipped over a bridge, crashed into
the ravine below, and severed her spinal cord.

I met Eva at a Fellowship of Christian Athletes (FCA) summer camp attended by almost a thousand girls a few years after her accident and, like most everyone else, I was captivated by her vivacious, good-natured beauty. She absolutely leaked joy! We bonded by instigating mostly innocent camp mischief, our shared affection for anything deep-fried, and our similar, booming laughs over the summers that followed. After we both graduated from college, she was hired to be on full-time staff with FCA in North Carolina, and I was hired to be on full-time staff with FCA in Tennessee, which gave us the opportunity to collaborate and run the same camps that had been part of our inspiration to pursue vocational ministry. Six years later, as a result of God's amazing sovereign grace, she fell in love with a Kentucky gentleman named Andrew Self, got married, and moved to his hometown, which is only an hour and a half north of me in Nashville, and that's when we really became thick as thieves!

Regardless of how busy our lives have been over the past thirty years, Eva and I have made herculean efforts to get together as often as we can, and those deep-talks-and-laughter-filled reunions are right up there at the top of my "happiest moments" list. However, every now and then during one of our special rendezvous, I have felt punched in the gut emotionally with the realization of the difficult moments my dear friend experiences as a result of being confined to a wheelchair.

One time not too long ago when we'd finagled our calendars and managed to carve out an entire day just to hang out, we went to lunch at a nice restaurant with an impressive variety of delicious food. Unfortunately, their lovely ambience and impressive menu were offset by the ignorance of our waiter who refused to look at Eva and even waved his hand dismissively in her direction while asking me in a bored voice, "And what will *she* be having?" as if the fact that her legs don't work meant her mind doesn't either. After enjoying a leisurely meal—during which I informed our waiter with a smile that Eva was not mentally or hearing impaired, but she was a math whiz who'd be the one figuring out our tip—we drove to a mall to do some back-to-school shopping for our kids.

Right about the time we'd gotten everything organized and ready to schlep inside from her specially equipped van, another driver came flying into the space next to the handicapped spot where we'd parked. The car pulled in so close and crooked that there was no room for Eva's mechanized ramp to unfold. I politely asked the driver of that car if she would back out and pull into the middle of her parking spot so that my friend could exit her van in a wheelchair. Instead of complying, she raced toward the mall like a fireman headed toward flames and yelled over her shoulder dismissively, "Sorry, but I'm in a real hurry!"

It took awhile for us to disassemble everything and move to another handicapped parking spot—of course, it took even longer than normal with all that paperwork the policeman made me fill out after I admitted to gouging Miss-Rushed-and-Rude's side door with my glass fingernail file (just kidding, but the thought did cross my mind, and I had to really deliberate whether or not to frisk it!). When we *finally* rolled into the mall toward the elevator, we discovered it was out of order and had to go all the way to the opposite side of the massive shopping center to access a working elevator in order get to the stores where we wanted to shop. Then to add insult to injury, the rude waiter must have relatives who work in retail because we ran into more of his obnoxious attitude in several department stores. In one store, a salesgirl pulled me aside and sniffed, "Will you please watch her? Because I really don't want her wheels running over any of our clothes and getting them dirty."

Later that afternoon when we were sitting on a bench enjoying our decadent whole milk mochas with whipped cream (usually we both drink nonfat mochas, but we decided to splurge that day), I tried to explain how sorry I was about the prejudice and obstacles she had to deal with because she isn't ambulatory. How unfair it is that she'd been an innocent teenaged *victim*— she was the one who'd been severely injured by a reckless driver who didn't even have the decency to stop and admit the accident was their fault—yet some yahoos still treat her like a second-class citizen simply because she rolls instead of walks. But I didn't get more than a few sentences out before I started crying and got all emotional and emphatically declared, "I *hate* that you're stuck in that chair!"

At which point my dear friend began consoling *me*. She sincerely thanked me for being grieved on her behalf. Then she said gently, "Lisa, I used to hate being stuck in this wheelchair, too. I used to have bitterness toward the driver who ran me off the road. I was humiliated by how some people regarded me with pity or condescension, and I was depressed about my physical limitations. But I don't resent this life anymore. As a matter of fact, I now consider all of it to be a gift. I'm grateful that God found me *worthy* to be in this chair because it's allowed me to have a life so much bigger than I would have had without it. Without this chair, I would've married my high school sweetheart and probably gotten a job at the cotton mill in the tiny town I grew up in just like my mom and dad. I wouldn't have gone to college. I wouldn't have had the opportunity to be on stages all over the country and talk about Jesus. So I wouldn't have met Andrew, and we wouldn't have our girls. God has done so much more than just give me tolerance for my situation—He's actually brought me to a place of thanksgiving."

Frisking our thoughts and changing our position can do wonders when it comes to rocking us out of mental and emotional ruts and getting us back on the highway of happy. We really can use our minds to turn our frowns upside down. However, *cultivating* happiness—that is tending and fertilizing our God-given joy so as to make it grow bigger and bloom more often—requires *intentional gratitude*. And deliberate thankfulness—the kind Eva radiates—delivers a double blessing because *gratitude is both the fertilizer and the fruit of happiness*. Gratitude *leads* us toward happiness and it *flows* from happiness.

A wonderful example of intentional gratitude took place when Jesus and His disciples were traveling to Jerusalem along a route bordering the rancorous regions of Samaria and Galilee, and suddenly a gang of rough-looking guys began shouting at Him from across the street. These ten men who were hoping for a miracle came face-to-face with the Messiah:

> Now on his way to Jerusalem, Jesus traveled along the border between Samaria and Galilee. As he was going into a village, ten men who had leprosy met him. They stood at a distance and called out in a loud voice, "Jesus, Master, have pity on us!"
>
> When he saw them, he said, "Go, show yourselves to the priests." And as they went, they were cleansed.
>
> One of them, when he saw he was healed, came back, praising God in a loud voice. He threw himself at Jesus' feet and thanked him—and he was a Samaritan.
>
> Jesus asked, "Were not all ten cleansed? Where are the other nine? Has no one returned to give praise to God except this foreigner?" Then he said to him, "Rise and go; your faith has made you well." (Luke 17:11–19 NIV)

Even from a distance, I'm sure Jesus and the twelve knew they were lepers. Anyone could've made that assessment because, according to Old Testament law, whoever was afflicted with leprosy—the oldest disease in recorded history[1]—was compelled to yell, "Unclean, unclean," whenever they were out in public so as to keep others from being infected with their terrible, highly contagious disease.[2]

It was also mandatory for them to wear torn, ragged clothes and unkempt hair—probably just in case someone was hard of hearing and didn't notice their self-incriminatory "Unclean, unclean" cries. During the first century, lepers were hard to miss and easy to marginalize—pretty much the lowest people on society's totem pole. They were literally and figuratively quarantined. Ostracized. Denounced. Strongly discouraged from even a fraction of fraternization with "normal" folk. I can't even imagine how emotionally debilitating that kind of stigmatization was for them.

Based on medical records, their physical debilitation is quantifiable, as author Ken Gire explains:

> It's a horrible disease, leprosy. It begins with little specks on the eyelids and on the palms of the hand. Then it spreads over the body. It bleaches the hair white. It casts a cadaverous pallor over the skin, crusting it with scales and erupting over it with oozing sores.
>
> But that's just what happens on the surface. Penetrating the skin the disease, like a moth, eats its way through the network of nerves woven throughout the body's tissues. Soon the body becomes numb to the point of sensory deprivation, numbed to both pleasure and pain. A toe can

break, and it will register no pain. And sensing no pain, the leper will continue walking, only to worsen the break and hasten the infection. One by one the appendages of the leper suffer their fate against the hard edges of life.[3]

Dr. Paul Brand, one of the leading authorities on Hansen's disease (the modern medical term for leprosy) in the twenty-first century, described how patients at a leprosarium in India would reach directly into a fire to retrieve something they'd accidentally dropped, walk barefoot across broken glass, and work their fingers down to the bone as a result of their extreme nerve damage. Worse still, he documented numerous cases of sleeping patients losing portions of their fingers and toes to hungry rats during the night, which led to the rule that everyone released from the hospital after treatment for leprosy had to take home a cat for nocturnal protection.[4]

It's hard to imagine a worse plight, and so it makes sense why this motley crew was so desperate that they hollered, "Please have pity on us, Master!" to Jesus, a man they'd never met. By acknowledging Him as a teacher (the word *Master* actually means "rabbi"—in other words, a Jewish sage or scholar), they were obviously hoping He had enough knowledge to help them. But it also underscores the extremity of their desperation because ancient rabbis weren't reputed to be professional healers. They were noted for quoting Torah, sharing parables, and imparting wisdom, not medical miracles.

I can picture their shoulders drooping and all the hope draining from their faces when Jesus replied, "Go, show yourselves to the priests." Jesus' advice was in adherence to Jewish law (Lev. 14:1), but if you're familiar with other healing encounters described in the Gospels, this response was uncharacteristic of our typically personable and profoundly compassionate Savior. And my guess is at least one or two of the ten rolled their eyes and muttered something like, "We should've known this teacher dude would give some by-the-book response." His seemingly rote directive definitely wasn't what they were hoping to hear. They wanted a cure, not a class assignment. But for reasons Luke doesn't explain, they still obeyed Christ's command. Maybe it was the authoritative tone in His voice, or maybe they didn't think they had any other viable options. So they turned to head for the rectory, and in that moment, all ten were instantaneously and miraculously healed.

Can you imagine their surprise, excitement, and relief? Several of my friends have been pronounced cancer-free after long bouts with that disease, and those of us who love them almost pulled our hamstrings while jumping up and down and cheering ourselves hoarse as a result. I'm guessing these ten lepers reacted with the same kind of boisterous exuberance when they looked down at their supernaturally healed, baby-soft skin. They were probably acting like frat boys whose home team won the championship: chest bumps, kissing strangers, and hooting and hollering all the way down Main Street. However, according to Dr. Luke's

account of this first-century phenomenon, in all their revelry all
but one forgot to thank the Great Physician. Only one man spun
around, ran back to Jesus, threw himself down at Christ's dusty
incarnate feet, and said, "THANK YOU."

   . . . *and he was a Samaritan* (Luke 17:18b).

Which means this individual had suffered the social stigma
and emotional torment of being considered dirty long before he
became infected with leprosy. Thus, to say this poor fellow had a
double whammy of "hard" is a major understatement. He was from
the ultimate wrong side of the tracks and definitely didn't make
the football team or have anyone to sit next to in the lunchroom.
Regular pariahs wouldn't give him the time of day. I think he's the
one who remembered to thank Jesus for restoring him because he's
the one who most remembered how horrible his life had been. He
was *intentionally grateful* because he hadn't forgotten how disfig-
ured his life was before the Messiah graciously entered it.

———

Because I'm fifty-three and single, I often teasingly say, "My
husband is lost and won't stop to ask for directions." But the truth
of the matter is that the main reason I'm single is because I was
very broken and foolish in my twenties and thirties. Most of the
men I was attracted to were abusive in some way—largely because
of childhood trauma and sexual abuse, destructive personal relationships were my default setting for decades—so God protected

me from them. And the few kind, Christian men I dated for any length of time, God protected from me because I was such a romantic train wreck. It took me a really long time to recognize and admit I needed deep emotional healing, and by that time not only had I squandered the typical matrimony years of young adulthood, but I'd also missed the biological window of motherhood.

Now, please know I don't for a nanosecond believe our Creator Redeemer is capricious or punitive . . . He has been extraordinarily patient with my crooked heart, and I've got gobs of firsthand experience of what the psalmist sang about God's long fuse:

> The LORD is compassionate and gracious, slow to anger, abounding in love. (Ps. 103:8 NIV)

But I do believe there are consequences to sin, and the consequence of my relational toxicity was that I never trusted a man enough to marry him and never got to experience the miracle of pregnancy. So the fact that God not only withheld His anger over my fear and foolishness but also restored to me the years I'd allowed "locusts" to devour (Joel 2:25) by allowing me to become Missy's mom when I was fifty years old has left me intoxicated with gratitude.

I wake up almost every morning with the thought, *I can't believe this is the life He's given me. That He allows me to be her mama. I don't deserve to be a mother.* If I truly reaped what I'd sowed in intimate human relationships, I'd be a shriveled-up old spinster with a houseful of cats who never got the opportunity to put together a complicated, knuckle-busting trampoline in the waning hours of Christmas Eve after her darling daughter had gone to sleep. And I hope I never forget that either. Because like the Samaritan leper, remembering what God saved me *from* keeps me moving *forward* toward Jesus with a heart full of thanksgiving and an I-can't-believe-I-won-the-lottery smile on my face. It's also becoming increasingly apparent to me that the more genuine thankfulness I express, the happier Missy is. So intentional gratitude really is the gift that keeps on giving!

———

In 2000, the Templeton Foundation funded a small group of experts to study the "science" of gratitude. Late philanthropist Sir John Templeton, who prompted the project, memorably proclaimed, "When we fill our minds with blessings and gratitude, an inner shift in consciousness can occur. As we focus on the abundance of our lives rather than what we lack, a wonderful blueprint for the future begins to emerge."[5] The resulting research uncovered a plethora of proof, linking gratitude with overall well-being, such as:

- People with higher gratitude levels show more activity in the hypothalamus, which leads to improved sleep, less physical discomfort, and lower stress and anxiety.[6]

- People who count their blessings on a regular basis (daily or weekly) report fewer aches and pains and better sleep than people who focus more on life's burdens.[7]
- Gratitude in the workplace increases both productivity and happiness.[8]
- Gratitude was a major contributor to resilience following the terrorist attacks in America on September 11, 2001.[9]

And my favorite observation regarding the link between intentional gratitude and tangible well-being is found in Randy Alcorn's recent book, *Happiness*—which I cannot recommend highly enough:

Before church, I sometimes speak with a man who has faced difficult life circumstances: his son died, he has battled cancer, he lost his job, and he's feeling the pains of old age. But the smile on his face is genuine. He speaks of the goodness of God and how grateful he is for Jesus, his Savior. He's a truly happy man. I enter the church service feeling I've already met with the Lord and heard a great message, all from my encounter with this brother.

One weekend I walked through the church parking lot and asked another man how he was doing. He launched into a litany of complaints that continued through the hallways and foyer as we headed to worship. He was profoundly unhappy. He answered my question honestly. But just because a perspective is transparently shared doesn't mean it isn't in dire need of adjustment.

These two men taught me a lesson I've seen thousands of times: with gratitude, there's happiness; without it, there's unhappiness. Every time.[10]

There's no time like the present to cultivate your happy. I strongly encourage you to use the lines below to begin basic gratitude inventory! All you have to do is answer this question: *Who and what are you thankful for today?*

_____

_____

_____

_____

_____

_____

_____

_____

_____

The Practical Pursuit of Happiness

1. What former "mess" has God transformed into what you now consider a miracle in your life?

   _____

   _____

   _____

2. What current hardship are you genuinely thankful for?

   _____

   _____

   _____

3. How have you experienced the double blessing of gratitude that is both the fertilizer and the fruit of happiness?

   _____

   _____

   _____

4. Reread Psalm 103:8. Where specifically has God been exceptionally patient with you lately?

   _____

   _____

   _____

5. Who is the most grateful person you know and how do they demonstrate a posture of thanksgiving?

_____

_____

_____

6. What do you think about Randy Alcorn's statement, "Just because a perspective is transparently shared doesn't mean it isn't in dire need of adjustment"? Describe a recent situation where you resembled this statement!

_____

_____

_____

7. What/who would those who know you best consider the most surprising entrant on your gratitude inventory?

_____

_____

_____

CHAPTER
NINE

Can Happy Change the World?

*If we grasp how happiness-saturated Scripture is, it
will radically affect our perspective as God's children
and greatly expand our outreach to the world.*[1]
Randy Alcorn

LAST FALL I HAD THE PRIVILEGE OF GOING TO
Thessaloniki, Greece, for the second time with my dear friend,
Christine Caine. And I brought along several of my closest friends
from Nashville so as to introduce them to A21, the incredibly
effective anti-human trafficking organization that Chris founded
with her husband, Nick. Since I'd been to Greece with Chris and
Nick the previous year, I knew what to expect. I knew our hearts

were going to be filleted when we spent time with women who'd been rescued from the sex trade and were now recovering in one of A21's safe houses for survivors on the outskirts of Thessaloniki. I knew we wouldn't be able to "unsee" what we observed as we drove through the red-light district late at night and witnessed lecherous men with their arms draped possessively around skinny, hollow-eyed, scantily clad teenaged girls. I knew that as a result of their introduction to A21, my friends would become as committed as I am about bringing awareness to this horrifying, exploitive, brutalizing widespread rape of human beings—which politicians and policing agencies have established is now more profitable than drug trafficking—and strive to put a stop to it on our watch.

But what none of us knew while planning the trip was that the greatest refugee crisis since World War II would be taking place just a few hours from our hotel in Greece. Hundreds, sometimes thousands, of mostly Syrian men, women, and children were washing up on the shores of the Greek island of Lesbos every single day because of its proximity to Turkey and Syria on the northern shore of the Aegean Sea; they were fleeing their country's violent war and the cruel oppression of ISIS extremists. When we heard the UN was desperate for volunteers to help with the unprecedented influx of refugees, we unanimously agreed to pile into vans and drive several hours to a remote, abandoned train-station-turned-tent-city that was serving as the second official stop for refugees after they were processed by the Greek government at Lesbos. Many had fled their homes with only the clothes on their backs, and some even lost loved ones in their frantic quest for asylum. On their perilous journey across the Aegean Sea, merciless pirates, using inflatable life rafts suitable for no more than twenty people, often crammed over one hundred passengers (all of whom were charged exorbitant "transport" fees) onto each raft so as to increase their profits. Many refugees—especially children—have drowned as a result.

There aren't words to adequately describe the hopelessness of the first group of refugees we watched climb out of buses a few hundred yards away from where we were asked to wait behind folding tables and then quickly assess only the most urgent needs of each individual or family. Once assessed, we were supposed to direct them to a makeshift medical tent where they could receive basic triage, or a clothing tent where they could sort through piles of donated clothes (to replace the lightweight attire that was tattered from their journey and not at all suitable for the bitterly cold temperatures in which they now found themselves), or to the dispiritingly long line for the food tent, or the "waiting" tent for those who'd been cleared to travel north into Macedonia. It was all we could do not to sob as we watched wave after wave of disheveled and exhausted men, women, and children trudge toward us. When we discussed the experience later, our group realized the disturbing mental image that immediately sprang to the front of all our minds was that of old photographs we'd seen of Jews shuffling pitiably toward Nazi concentration camps more than half a century earlier.

But we didn't have time to cry at that point because we were quickly overwhelmed by a crush of people begging for help. In short order, we shifted into Steel Magnolia mode and amended the slow and ineffective "sorting system" and began passing out food rations to everyone within reach; we gave formula to all the parents for their starving babies and teased with a rag-tag crew of rambunctious, flirtatious teenaged boys (young enough to be our *sons*) who were hungry for some small sense of normalcy amidst the trauma and sensed that a group of bossy female volunteers from America might be just the place to find it.

By far the most effective "aid" we handed out during those October evenings in 2015 happened when we got transferred to the children's tent. Hundreds of beautiful but apprehensive kids were gathered, flanked by their worried mamas and daddies; men and women who felt they had no choice but to leave behind their war-ravaged homeland and militant jihadists, yet knew what their children had already witnessed in the pursuit of safety and a better way of life may well have caused them permanent emotional damage.

Because there were no video games or toys to entertain those darling kids and none of us could speak their Middle Eastern dialects, we began singing and dancing a very animated version of the Hokey Pokey as a last resort. Unbeknownst to us, the Hokey Pokey is a universal favorite and, almost immediately, the refugee children formed a giant circle with the "crazy American chicks" and began singing and dancing their little hearts out, too.

We just might have set a Guinness Book world record for the length of time we danced to the Hokey Pokey there on the frigid border of Greece and Macedonia. Those precious peanuts were tireless; when one of us stopped to catch our breath, they'd pull on our sleeves and plead for us to keep going in lilting accents we couldn't understand but with adorable, upturned faces that were impossible to refuse. When I stepped out of the cacophonous ring of hokey-pokiers to take off my heavy sweatshirt, a young Muslim mom in a full burka approached shyly and asked, "May I speak with you for a moment?" in perfect English.

I said, "Yes, of course."

And was then completely caught off guard when she took my hands in hers, looked into my eyes, and said with a quiet smile, "Thank you so much for dancing with my son. His little sister was killed a few weeks before we left Syria, and he's been despondent ever since. This is the first time I've seen him laugh in a long time. My husband and I are so grateful to you."

She continued by saying she knew we were Christians—followers of Jesus Christ—and she believed our prayers to be powerful. Then she humbly asked if I would mind praying for her son's joy to return. I told her I'd be honored and asked for her permission to invoke the name of Jesus while I prayed for him. She considered my request solemnly for a few seconds before nodding graciously. I've prayed hundreds of thousands, if not millions, of prayers in my lifetime, but few have felt more sacred than when I got to lay my right hand on Abdulla's head, while holding Farema's hand with my left and pray for Jesus to mend her little man's broken heart.

Your initial response to the question "Can happy change the world?" might have been an eye-rolling, *That's doubtful.* Mine would've been a few years ago, too. But not anymore. Not since I've seen the redemptive effect this *glorious good news of the happy God* (1 Tim. 1:11) of which we've been entrusted has on those who have every reason to be joyless.

—

In chapter 4, we established that the theology of happy is first God-focused and then others-focused:

> In everything I have given you an example of how, by working hard like this, you must help the weak, remembering the words of the Lord Yeshua himself, *"There is more happiness in giving than in receiving."* (Acts 20:35 CJB, emphasis mine)

With that understanding, it shouldn't surprise us that there's an orthopraxy—a correct *practice* or *action*—connected with God's gift of pleasure, contentment, and fulfillment. But it may be surprising to find out there's once again a scientifically proven foundation that upholds the connection between happiness and others-centered generosity. For instance:

- Others-oriented compassion decreases stress hormones and inflammation, improves immune function, and decreases anxiety and depression.[2]
- Compassion increases the likelihood of longevity.[3]
- Compassionate working environments not only increase employee's overall productivity and wellbeing but also their *client's* well-being and satisfaction.[4]
- In children as young as two, happiness spikes higher when *giving* treats than when receiving them.[5]
- Cross-culturally and across socio-demographic groups, people who are compassionate are happier and more fulfilled.[6]

The data compiled in the above research didn't specify *how* to extend compassion, only that the acts had to be motivated by altruism and not self-serving (e.g., a man who steps in to help an elderly woman across a busy street only to impress his girlfriend). So our world-changing orthopraxy of happy may involve traveling to a Third World country on a mission/humanitarian trip *or* traveling across town to drive a friend to their chemo appointment. It might involve a big investment of financial resources like underwriting an orphan's life-saving surgery *or* giving away genuine smiles to those who feel invisible. It might be choosing to invest your time to help build a Habitat for Humanity home as a family over spring break *or* it might only take a few minutes to stop and engage a homeless person in conversation before pressing a few dollars into their palm.

The ongoing practice of others-oriented kindness and generosity will look different for all of us, but there are a couple of tools that will come in handy in *everyone's* compassion carryall:

World-Changing Habits of Happiness

Listen Intently

One of my favorite healing stories in the Gospels occurs when Jesus encounters a woman who's been hemorrhaging for *twelve* years (Mark 5:21–34). Mark explains that she's lost both her health and her wealth:

> In the crowd was a woman who had been sick for twelve years with a hemorrhage. She had suffered much from many doctors through the years and had become poor from paying them, and was no better but, in fact, was worse. (vv. 25–26 TLB)

Theologians concur that because of the nature of her illness and Old Testament ceremonial law, she also lost the joy of close human interaction. Miraculously, the blood flow stopped and her body was instantaneously healed when she reached out and touched the tassels on the edge of our Redeemer's robe:

> For she thought to herself, "If I can just touch his clothing, I will be healed." And sure enough, as soon as she had

touched him, the bleeding stopped and she knew she was well! (vv. 28–29 TLB)

Her interaction with the Great Physician could've/should've ended right there because she'd gotten what she came for: physical healing. Plus, Jesus was en route to Jairus's house, a leader in the community, to attend to his dying daughter (vv. 22–24). But instead, Jesus stops in the middle of a seemingly more important mission just to listen to her:

> The woman, knowing that she was healed, came and fell at Jesus' feet. Shaking with fear, she told him the *whole truth*. (v. 33 NCV, emphasis mine)

I believe Jesus stopped because, despite her medical cure, He knew her heart still needed care after twelve long years of suffering. So the Lamb of Judah paused for a moment to lean in and listen to one lonely woman's entire story.

Really listening—leaning in and giving our full attention to what someone else is communicating or attempting to communicate—is one of humanity's most powerful expressions of compassion. Unfortunately, in our digitized, hyperstimulated, selfie and social-media obsessed culture, being actively present while someone else tells their true, unfiltered story seems to be going the way of the Dodo bird. I'm sure, like me, you've found yourself awkwardly trailing off and not finishing a complete thought because the person in front of you stopped paying attention as soon as their phone started vibrating. Leisurely, device-less conversation between two people seems to becoming passé.

One of the happiest and healthiest listening experiences I've had recently happened after being invited by Jessie, the leader of an Alcoholics Anonymous group, to sit in on several of her meetings because of my mentoring relationship with a few women in the program. After calling the meeting to order and asking us to bow our heads for her beautifully articulated invocation, Jessie bellowed, "Okay, now y'all need to put those phones away because y'all *NEED TO HEAR* what your sistah's be saying or ain't none a y'all gonna be healed! And y'all bess not interrupt each ah-tha ee-tha or I'm gone bust y'all upside yo fat heads!"

My part of the deal in being allowed to attend Jessie's AA gatherings was that I wouldn't disclose anything shared during the meeting or speak during the meeting since I wasn't a recovering alcoholic. However, she didn't tell me I couldn't get tickled, for which I was very grateful, because I burst out laughing over her listening parameters! And I wholeheartedly endorse them, too. Honestly, I think the whole world would benefit if we'd all practice putting down our phones and not interrupting whoever's speaking . . . unless they're a windbag like me and you're about to miss an appointment or something.

Look People in the Eyes

You've probably heard the familiar adage: "The eyes are the windows to the soul," but did you know it's true? Research shows we can actually read someone else's emotions by gazing into their eyes.[7]

In *The Happiness Track,* Dr. Seppälä explains how empathy research data has been gleaned by asking participants to look at photographs only revealing someone's eyes and describe the subject's emotion. And participants were able to accurately describe the emotion portrayed based on the angle of their eyebrows and the creases on the side of their eyes.[8]

One of the habits I've been teaching Missy from day one is to look people in the eyes when they talk to her or she's talking to them. When my little girl is being praised, taught, nurtured, or reprimanded by an adult relative, caregiver, or authority figure, I'm teaching her that making eye contact is a sign of respect and relationship. When she's engaging with her friends, I'm teaching her that making eye contact is a sign of respect and relationship. And when she doesn't know—or isn't particularly fond of—the adult or child she's interacting with, I'm teaching her to make eye contact *anyway.* When she asked me a few weeks ago why she had to make eye contact and be "is-is-spectful" with a certain ornery boy in her Sunday school class, I told her that just like everybody else he is an image-bearer of God and therefore worthy of respect, whether he'd smeared the glitter-glue stick on her picture of Moses or not!

Eye contact is a big deal in our family because I believe it's difficult to have a deep connection with someone else without it. You can have a superficial conversation or endure a lecture or make a monologue without eye contact, but it's hard to have a genuine, heart-to-heart connection that *matters*. And as image-bearers of a perfectly relational God, we're all wired for this type of connection.

Several months ago, as I was nearing the end of a very long book-signing line at the end of a very long conference, I noticed a young woman who'd been waiting to speak with me. After thirty-plus years of teaching ministry, I'm still hugely honored and slightly discombobulated that anybody besides my mom or a bill collector would actually wait in line to talk to me or ask me to sign something. But on this particular day, I was just flat worn-out. I'd taught four sessions in a row, had been wearing "two-hour-heels" for about ten hours, and my compression undergarments were kind of cutting off my circulation, so all I really wanted to do was hobble back to the hotel, change into pajamas, and channel surf. But I could tell she'd been crying, so when she approached me, I looked her in the eyes and asked gently, "Honey, would you like to tell me what happened that broke your heart?" And that's when her walls came tumbling down.

It took her well over an hour to describe the torment she'd suffered from early childhood through high school. The abandonment by her father—incarcerated before she was born. The physical abuse by her mother—addicted to crack cocaine and men who cracked ribs with their fists. The sexual molestation by multiple men, closely related to her. The bullying by kids—classmates who mocked her second-hand clothes and self-conscious stutter.

About midway through her torrent of sorrow, I led her to a bench in the church foyer so she could be more comfortable and I could take my hateful shoes off. But I didn't dare take my eyes off hers as she continued to expel wave after wave of the emotion she'd bottled up for years.

That first conversation with my new friend led to several more. Since that time, she's been enveloped into a nurturing small group at her church and is slowly but surely healing under the loving care of a safe community. I saw her at another event a few weeks ago where she told me she'd like to speak with me privately again but winked and said she promised not to wipe her nose on my shirt this time. It seemed fitting to find another bench where, once again, we sat down facing each other. Then she confided softly, "Miss Lisa, thank you for the way you treated me while I fell apart telling you my story when we first met. The way you looked me in the eyes and let me finish made me feel like I mattered. And I don't think I've mattered much to very many people in my whole life until here lately."

It's an exquisite privilege to peek in the window of someone else's soul, isn't it?

Love Hard, Even When It Is Hard

I lost two adoption attempts before beginning the arduous process with Missy; the second one left me reeling like a punch-drunk boxer. Friends who've experienced both late-term miscarriages and failed adoptions tell me the grief is similar. That both losses leave a similar-shaped hole in your heart and mind. I only know I felt like I'd been hit by a semi afterwards. Like the wind had been knocked out of me and I couldn't catch my emotional breath.

It probably sounds masochistic that it was only a few weeks after my second adoption attempt failed when I said yes after a friend called, explained about this very sick toddler in Haiti who desperately needed someone to stand in the gap for her, then asked if I was willing. Of course, I knew it was probable that my battered soul would get pummeled to smithereens again, but I was oddly at peace about it most days of our two-year, roller-coaster trek. And now that Missy's been home for longer than I waited and prayed I'd get to be her second mama, I've realized the pain of parenthood will continue until I take my last breath or Jesus splits the sky riding a white horse. Because the biggest chunk of my heart is now wandering around outside of my chest and attached to her. However, I've also come to realize that I prefer it out there as opposed to being sealed up on some lonely, self-protective shelf. Motherhood has been the hardest love I've ever fought for in my life, and my only regret is that I didn't begin slugging away for it sooner.

Now I'd rather forego carbohydrates than winnow my favorite C. S. Lewis quotes down to just one. That's saying a lot since I think hot rosemary bread dredged in olive oil and chips dunked in queso pretty much make the world go round. But if *forced* to choose a single of Sir Lewis's citations to hang my hat on, it would have to be this one:

> Love anything, and your heart will certainly be wrung and positively broken. If you want to make sure of keeping it intact, you must give your heart to no one, not even to an animal. Wrap it carefully round with hobbies and little luxuries; avoid all entanglements; lock it up safe in the casket or coffin of your selfishness. But in that casket—safe, dark, motionless, airless—it will change. It will not be broken; it will become unbreakable, impenetrable, irredeemable. The alternative to tragedy, or at least to the risk of tragedy, is damnation.[9]

If we will choose to love hard, even when it *is* hard, I'm willing to bet all the hot bread and tortilla chips of my future on the fact that our planet will be a much better—much *happier*—place to live.

The Practical Pursuit of Happiness

1. What human tragedy—in your community, nation, or globally—has been impossible for you to "unsee"?

_____

_____

_____

2. What have you done about the God-given unrest you have regarding this particular human tragedy?

_____

_____

_____

3. How has someone handed you tangible joy when your arms were so full of grief you weren't sure you'd ever smile again?

_____

_____

_____

4. What's your favorite thing—time, money, or heartfelt affection—to give away?

_____

_____

_____

5. What do you find most difficult to give generously—time, money, or heartfelt affection?

_____

_____

_____

6. Who has consistently shown you compassion simply by listening to you intently? Have you ever thanked them for their investment in your life?

_____

_____

_____

7. What "hard love" have you fought tooth and nail for?

_____

_____

_____

CHAPTER TEN

Is There Happily Ever After?

*We are not just going to heaven, we're
heading for our wedding celebration and
marriage to the Lamb of God, Jesus.*[1]
Scotty Smith

THE LAST FEW MONTHS HAVE BEEN TOO BUSY—WE WERE
on the road twenty-seven out of thirty days recently—so when
we finally returned home, I was beyond thrilled at the promise
of sleeping in my own bed. As soon as we got home from the
airport, we took an evening stroll around our property to stretch
our legs. I couldn't help smiling as I listened to Missy's chatter
and watched Cookie charge joyfully through thickets of woods

and fields trying to catch one of the countless rabbits that claim our hilly five-acre "farmette" as their home. Cookie is the sweetest dog I've ever had, but she's kind of a klutz, and watching those wily bunnies outwit her is a constant source of amusement on our ambling adventures. On our way back up the steep driveway toward the house, I mused contently, *Cookie's antics while the sun was setting behind her here in our little corner of the world is the perfect prelude to what will surely be a great night's sleep at* home!

But my contentment was hijacked at two o'clock in the morning when I was jarred awake by a loud noise that sounded like one of the logs had just fallen off our house. I sat up in bed, trying to get my bearings in my darkened bedroom, and noticed Cookie's outline standing over what looked to be a very big frog. Only it wasn't. It was a very dead bunny. It became startlingly apparent that while she was galloping goofily through the woods out of our sight on our stroll a few hours earlier, she'd actually *caught* one of those darling little critters, which had been enthusiastically regurgitated on my white cowhide rug. Sometimes you just can't win for snoozing, can you?

The Already but Not Yet

Canceled flights, jeans that no longer button, and rummaging through laundry room cabinets in search of carpet cleaner in the middle of the night because of our naughty pooch are just a few of the most recent hardships that have reminded me our little log home here on a hill in Tennessee isn't heaven. But even the happiest days here—when Missy is singing and dancing, and Cookie is chasing rabbits, *not* eating them!—won't come close to the *flawless fulfillment* we'll experience when our Creator Redeemer calls us to our final happy place. That's Paul's point in his first letter to the early Christians living in Corinth:

> Now we see a dim reflection, as if we were looking into a mirror, but then we shall see clearly. *Now I know only a part, but then I will know fully*, as God has known me. (1 Cor. 13:12 NCV, emphasis mine)

It is also the overriding theme of Jesus' announcement in the latter part of John's gospel account:

> "Don't let this throw you. You trust God, don't you? Trust me. There is plenty of room for you in my Father's home. If that weren't so, would I have told you that I'm on my way to get a room ready for you? And if I'm on my way to get your room ready, *I'll come back and get you so you can live where I live*. And you already know the road I'm taking." (John 14:1–4, MSG, emphasis mine)

The book of Hebrews also begins by tipping its hat to what's ahead for God's people:

> Long ago, *at many times* and *in many ways*, God spoke to our fathers by the prophets, but in *these last days* he has spoken to us by his Son, whom he appointed the heir of

all things, through whom also he created the world. He is the radiance of the glory of God and the exact imprint of his nature, and he upholds the universe by the word of his power. After making purification for sins, he sat down at the right hand of the Majesty on high, having become as much superior to angels as the name he has inherited is more excellent than theirs. (Heb. 1:1–4 ESV, emphasis mine)

God spoke through prophets like Isaiah and Elijah. He also spoke through signs and dreams, as evidenced in the Old Testament books of Daniel and Job. Our heavenly Father used a flaming topiary to direct Moses. He even condescended to communicate with people through the Urim and Thummim, which were basically holy dice used to discern His will. Remember how the disciples "cast lots" to replace Judas in Acts 1? They were probably using Urim and Thummim, holy stones that were used for divination.

So the pastor of Hebrews acknowledges that Jehovah spoke at *many times*—*polymeros* in Greek—using *many ways*—*polytropos* in Greek. Then in verse 2 he proclaims that the period of history in which they were living was the period of the *last days*. This phrase, which is sometimes translated "the latter days," is significant. When it's used in New Testament literature, it always refers to the time period between the first coming of Jesus Christ and His imminent return, which means we're in the last days right now—it is occurring in *our lifetime*!

It's what Pete (my affectionate, albeit informal, nickname for Peter) was preaching about at Pentecost when he quoted Joel and said God would pour out His Spirit in the *last days*. The last days means we're living in *the already but not yet*—humanity has already witnessed the first coming of Jesus Christ. And if you've put your hope in His sacrificial death on the cross and subsequent resurrection, you are *already* reconciled to God. The debt of your sin has been completely paid. However, we're *not yet* glorified. This spinning planet is not our true home. One day Jesus will come a second time . . . He'll split the sky wide open while riding a white horse (Mark 13; Revelation 19) and He'll escort us, His bride, to heaven where there will be no more crying and no more dying, and our pleasure, contentment, and fulfillment will be *perfected*. But we're not there yet.

The guy I plan on gabbing with a lot when we finally get to heaven, Sir C. S. Lewis (whom you've probably noticed I have a small platonic crush on), puts a poignant spin on why our happy can't be perfect *here* lest we stop longing for *there*:

> The settled happiness and security which we all desire, God withholds from us by the very nature of the world: but joy, pleasure, and merriment, He has scattered broadcast. We are never safe, but we have plenty of fun, and some ecstasy. It is not hard to see why. The security we crave would teach us to rest our hearts in this world and oppose an obstacle to our return to God: a few moments of happy love, a landscape, a symphony, a merry meeting

with our friends, a bathe or a football match, have no such tendency. Our Father refreshes us on the journey with some pleasant inns, but will not encourage us to mistake them for home.[2]

In other words, God graciously allows us a sacrament of happy *here*, but it's a pale imitation of the immutable, immaculate happiness we'll have *there*.

———

The Emerging Expectancy

> *That is what makes life at once so splendid and so strange. . . . The true happiness is that we don't fit. We come from somewhere else. We have lost our way.*[3]
> G. K. Chesterton

Once we begin to understand the dichotomy of this *already but not yet* era we're living in, which Chesterton poetically described as a sort of exiled state or "wrong star," then we mature to a state of spiritual understanding I like to call *the emerging expectancy*.

During the two years it took to bring Missy home from Haiti, I grew more and more anxious for our adoption to be finalized. Every time I got to be with her was like Christmas morning. The more I got to know her, the more I became attached to this precious child who, God willing, would become my daughter. I was tickled to discover more and more affinities we shared. Like the fact that she liked her meals on the spicy side. Her favorite snack became the almonds sprinkled with sea salt I brought with me on visits. Her favorite music on my iPod included the songs with a pronounced, percussive beat. She arranged the things around her as neat and tidy as possible . . . even in the chaos of the orphanage. She liked her bedcovers untucked at night, so she could wiggle her feet freely. And she was an enthusiastic dancer with excellent rhythm (okay, so this one's only half true for me).

As you can imagine, our good-byes became increasingly difficult, and my desire to see her again became stronger and stronger until it was a palpable ache. A literal longing to be reunited with this child I'd grown to love more deeply than I knew was possible. Toward the end of our journey (more than a year and a half into the arduous adoption process), I was told by an official in Haiti that because of some politically motivated changes in the department that oversees child welfare, I might not get to bring Missy home after all. This led to some very fervent prayers for God's favor and intervention, as well as a quiet resolve that if it didn't work out for me to bring her here, He'd make a way for me to move there. I figured since God had totally changed the topography of my heart to become a parent, plus her need for an advocate to survive, He'd make "us" work out one way or another! My expectancy to be her mama had emerged into a yearning that wouldn't be satiated by anything less.

Oh how much more you and I are made to crave being reunited with our adoptive heavenly Father, as Paul explains in Romans 8:

> We know that the whole creation has been groaning as in the pains of childbirth right up to the present time. Not only so, but we ourselves, who have the firstfruits of the Spirit, *groan inwardly as we wait eagerly for our adoption to sonship*, the redemption of our bodies. (vv. 22–23 NIV, emphasis mine)

The Flawless Fulfillment

When I was a kid, the heaven I heard about in Sunday school sounded like a fairy-tale kind of place, what with all the broad-winged angels sitting astride cotton-candy clouds and friendly musicians strolling on gilded streets. But the whole of Scripture reveals heaven to be an actual place, not an optimist's caricature. Although the vision of heaven (a.k.a.: The New Jerusalem) John describes in Revelation is so admittedly fantastical, it's hard for skeptics to swallow:

> He then carried me away in the Spirit to a great, high mountain and showed me the holy city, Jerusalem, coming down out of heaven from God, arrayed with God's glory. Her radiance was like a precious jewel, like a jasper stone, clear as crystal. The city had a massive high wall,

with twelve gates. Twelve angels were at the gates; the names of the twelve tribes of Israel's sons were inscribed on the gates. There were three gates on the east, three gates on the north, three gates on the south, and three gates on the west. The city wall had twelve foundations, and the twelve names of the twelve apostles of the Lamb were on the foundations.

The one who spoke with me had a gold measuring rod to measure the city, its gates, and its wall. The city is laid out in a square; its length and width are the same. He measured the city with the rod at 12,000 stadia. Its length, width, and height are equal. Then he measured its wall, 144 cubits according to human measurement, which the angel used. The building material of its wall was jasper, and the city was pure gold clear as glass. The foundations of the city wall were adorned with every kind of jewel: the first foundation is jasper, the second sapphire, the third chalcedony, the fourth emerald, the fifth sardonyx, the sixth carnelian, the seventh chrysolite, the eighth beryl, the ninth topaz, the tenth chrysoprase, the eleventh jacinth, the twelfth amethyst. The twelve gates are twelve pearls; each individual gate was made of a single pearl. The broad street of the city was pure gold, transparent as glass. (Rev. 21:10–21)

It's important for us to remember that the literary style in this prophetic book may very well be hyperbolic symbolism, which was commonly used in ancient Jewish writings as theologian and eschatological expert Bruce Metzger explains:

> The description is architecturally preposterous, and must not be taken with flat-footed literalism. In ancient time the cube was held to be the most perfect of all geometric forms. By this symbolism, therefore, John wants us to understand that the heavenly Jerusalem is absolutely splendid, with a harmony and symmetry of perfect proportions.[4]

And don't forget the Holy of Holies—that place where God's presence was once manifest in His temple here on the earth—measured twenty cubits by twenty cubits by twenty cubits (1 Kings 6:20), so it was a symmetric cube, too! Therefore, we can accurately surmise that John's vision of where we'll get to commune with Christ in glory was a place of complete *perfection*. Everything will be flawless, including our happiness. When Jesus returns for us and we get to waltz into "happy ever after" on His arm, the psalmist implies we won't have to nibble on dark chocolate for pleasure or cuddle with our kids for contentment or peruse God's Word for fulfillment because our souls will be entirely satisfied just by looking into our Bridegroom's face:

> And when I awake in heaven, *I will be fully satisfied,* for I will see you face-to-face. (Ps. 17:15b TLB, emphasis mine)

Isaiah confirms with a hearty amen:

They will enter Jerusalem with joy, *and their happiness will last forever. Their gladness and joy will fill them completely,* and sorrow and sadness will go far away. (Isa. 35:10b NCV, emphasis mine)

When I read those words, I can't help but think of my dear Tootsie-Roll-Pop daddy who never seemed *completely* happy in this life. One of the last coherent requests he made in the days leading up to his death a few years ago after bravely fighting colon cancer, which had cruelly metastasized to his lungs, was for us to change him into his "good" pajamas and a pair of slippers. My mom (who had miraculously reconciled with Dad during the last year of his life and became his dear friend and confidant), my sister, and I all three demurred because we were afraid that jostling him in his frail condition would cause too much pain. Plus, he was hooked up to several I.V. tubes for hydration, etc., which made the prospect of changing him even more daunting. But he was gruffly insistent. We assumed the morphine was making him more agitated than usual, so I gently explained our reticence and said, "Hey, Daddy, the pajamas you're wearing right now look fine. They're the ones Theresa and I gave you last year for Christmas, remember? And they're clean, Dad, I promise," which is when he fixed his blue eyes on mine and croaked firmly, "Lisa, I'm about to be dancing on streets of gold, and I do *not* want to go up there in old pajamas and bare feet."

Some days I'm convinced I hear Dad's carefree laughter in the wind as he revels in the *perfect* happiness that we can enjoy in part until God calls us home too!

> I heard a voice thunder from the Throne: "Look! Look! God has moved into the neighborhood, making his home with men and women! They're his people, he's their God. He'll wipe every tear from their eyes. Death is gone for good—tears gone, crying gone, pain gone—all the first order of things gone." The Enthroned continued, "Look! I'm making everything new. Write it all down—each word dependable and accurate." (Rev. 21:3–5 MSG)

The Practical Pursuit of Happiness

1. What recent comical catastrophe was a tangible reminder for you that this world isn't heaven?

_____

_____

_____

2. If you got to design your residence in glory, what would it look like?

_____

_____

_____

3. How would you paraphrase C. S. Lewis's quote, "Our Father refreshes us on the journey with some pleasant inns, but will not encourage us to mistake them for home"?

_____

_____

_____

4. What are your most pleasant inns currently? Have you ever felt like they had the power to diminish your longing for heaven?

_____

_____

_____

5. Reread Psalm 17:15b. What emotions stir when you imagine the future reality of actually being face-to-face with Jesus?

_____

_____

_____

6. Reread Isaiah 35:10b. How would you personalize Isaiah's prophecy as a journal entry?

_____

_____

_____

7. What's one practical step you can take to cultivate your expectancy about being perfectly reconciled and reunited with our Creator Redeemer in heaven?

_____

_____

_____

Notes

Chapter 1

1. Thomas A. Hand, *St. Augustine on Prayer* (South Bend, IN: Newman Press, 1963), 1.

2. Emma Seppälä, *The Happiness Track* (New York, NY: Harper Collins Publishers, 2016), 8.

3. Thomas Manton, "Twenty Sermons on Important Passages of Scripture," *The Complete Works of Thomas Manton*, vol. 2 (London: Forgotten Books, 2016).

4. Randy Alcorn, *Happiness* (Carol Stream, IL: Tyndale House Publishers, 2015), 8.

5. See www.dictionary.com.

6. Alcorn, *Happiness,* 19.

7. Tremper Longman III, *How to Read the Psalms* (Downers Grove, IL: InterVarsity, 1988), 45.

8. Robert L. Thomas, *New American Standard Hebrew-Aramaic and Greek Dictionaries: Updated Edition* (Anaheim, CA: Foundation Publications, Inc., 1998).

9. Spiro Zodhiates, ed., *Hebrew-Greek Key Word Study Bible* (Chattanooga, TN: AMG, 1996), 627, 1911.

10. *Strong's Greek Concordance*, #3107, http://biblehub.com/greek/3107.htm.

Chapter 2

1. Randy Alcorn, *Happiness* (Carol Stream, IL: Tyndale House Publishers, 2015), 107.
2. *Strong's Greek Concordance*, #2098, http://biblehub.com/greek/2098.htm.
3. John Piper, *The Pleasures of God* (Sisters, OR: Multnomah Publishers, 2000), 26.

Chapter 3

1. John Piper, *The Pleasures of God* (Sisters, OR: Multnomah Publishers, 2000), 50.

Chapter 4

1. Martin Seligman, *Flourish: A Visionary New Understanding of Happiness and Well-being* (New York, NY: Free Press, 2011).
2. Gretchen Rubin, *The Happiness Project* (New York, NY: Harper Collins Publishers, 2009).
3. Emma Seppälä, *The Happiness Track* (New York, NY: Harper Collins Publishers, 2016), 11–12.
4. Deborah K. Heisz, *Live Happy: Ten Practices for Choosing Joy* (New York, NY: Harper Collins Publishers, 2016), 13–15.
5. Robert A. Emmons and Michael McCullough, "Counting Blessings versus Burdens: An Experimental Investigation of Gratitude and Subjective Well-Being in Daily Life," *Journal of Personality and Social Psychology* 84, no. 2 (February 2003): 377–89, http://greatergood.berkeley.edu/pdfs/GratitudePDFs/6Emmons-BlessingsBurdens.pdf.
6. Laura D. Kubzansky, Laurie T. Martin, and Stephen L. Buka, "Early Manifestations of Personality and Adult Health: A Life Course Perspective," *Health Psychology* 28, no. 3 (May 2009): 364–72.

Chapter 5

1. "Fight Memory Loss with a Smile or Chuckle," *Science Daily*, April 27, 2014, http://www.sciencedaily.com/releases/ 2014/04/140427185149.itm; and Lee S. Berk and Stanley A. Tan, "[Beta]-Endorphin and HGH Increase Are Associated with Both the Anticipation and Experience of Mirthful Laughter," *FASEB Journal*, Supplement A382 (2006), http://www.fasej.org/cgi/content/ meeting_abstract/20/4/A382-b.

Chapter 6

1. Timothy Keller, *Walking with God through Pain and Suffering* (New York, NY: Dutton, 2013), 31.

Chapter 7

1. Sonja Lyubomirsky, *The How of Happiness: A Scientific Approach to Getting the Life You Want* (New York, NY: Penguin Books, 2007), 20–23.

2. Arnold Dallimore, *Spurgeon: A New Biography* (Edinburgh, UK: Banner of Truth, 1987), 186.

Chapter 8

1. Philip Yancey, *Where Is God When It Hurts?* (Grand Rapids, MI: Zondervan, 1998), 23.

2. Ben Witherington III, *The Gospel of Mark: A Socio-Rhetorical Commentary* (Grand Rapids, MI: Eerdmans, 2001), 102–3. See also Leviticus 13:45.

3. Ken Gire, *Moments with the Savior: A Devotional Life of Christ* (Grand Rapids, MI: Zondervan, 1998), 110–11.

4. Yancey, *Where Is God When It Hurts?*, 25–26.

5. Deborah K. Heisz, *Live Happy: Ten Practices for Choosing Joy* (New York, NY: Harper Collins Publishers, 2016), 142.

6. Ibid., 143.

7. Robert A. Emmons and Michael McCullough, "Counting Blessings versus Burdens: An Experimental Investigation of Gratitude and Subjective Well-Being in Daily Life," *Journal of Personality and Social Psychology* 84, no. 2 (February 2003): 377–89.

8. Emiliana R. Simon-Thomas and Jeremy Adam Smith, "How Grateful Are Americans?" January 10, 2013, http://greatergood.berkeley. edu/article/item/how_grateful_are_americans.

9. Barbara L. Fredrickson et al., "What Good Are Positive Emotions in Crisis? A Prospective Study of Resilience and Emotions Following the Terrorist Attacks on the United States on September 11th, 2001," *Journal of Personality and Social Psychology* 84, no. 2 (February 2003): 365–76.

10. Randy Alcorn, *Happiness* (Carol Stream, IL: Tyndale House Publishers, 2015), 362.

Chapter 9

1. Randy Alcorn, *Happiness* (Carol Stream, IL: Tyndale House Publishers, 2015), 260.

2. B. L. Fredrickson et al., "Open Hearts Build Lives: Positive Emotions, Induced Through Loving-Kindness, Meditation, Build Consequential Personal Resources," *Journal of Personality and Social Psychology* 95, no. 5 (2008): 1045–62.

3. J. Holt-Lunstad et al., "Social Relationships and Mortality Risk: A Meta-analytic Review," *PLoS Med.* 7, no. 7 (2010): 31000316, DOI: 10.137/journal.pmed.1000316.

4. Sigal G. Barsade and Olivia A. O'Neill, "What's Love Got to Do with It? A Longitudinal Study of the Culture of Compassionate Love

and Employee and Client Outcomes in the Long-Term Care Setting," *Administrative Science Quarterly* 20, no. 20 (2014): 1–48.

5. L. B. Aknin et al., "Giving Leads to Happiness in Young Children," *PLoS ONE* 7, no. 6 (2012): e:39211, DOI: 10.1371/journal. pone.0039211.

6. Emma Seppälä, *The Happiness Track* (New York, NY: Harper Collins Publishers, 2016), 151.

7. Simon Baron-Cohen et al., "The 'Reading the Mind in the Eyes' Test Revised Version: A Study with Normal Adults, and Adults with Asperger Syndrome or High-Functioning Autism," *Journal of Child Psychology and Psychiatry* 42, no. 2 (2001): 241–51.

8. Seppälä, *The Happiness Track*, 362–63.

9. C. S. Lewis, *The Four Loves* (New York, NY: Harcourt, 1960), 121.

Chapter 10

1. Scotty Smith and Michael Card, *Unveiled Hope* (Nashville, TN: Thomas Nelson Publishers, 1997), 185.

2. C. S. Lewis, *The Problem of Pain* (New York, NY: Macmillan, 1962), 115.

3. *The G. K. Chesterton Collection* (London, UK: Catholic Way Publishing, 2014), e-book.

4. Bruce M. Metzger, *Breaking the Code* (Nashville, TN: Abingdon Press, 1993), 101.

The Gospel of Mark

THE JESUS WE'RE ACHING FOR

LISA HARPER

CONTENTS

INTRODUCTION

Since Missy's been home from Haiti for almost two years and is a whopping six years old, I recently added some simple chores to her daily routine so as to help her develop character, a sense of responsibility, and sow some work ethic seeds. For instance, now when we come home from a Target run (you know the ones when you planned on just picking up laundry detergent yet somehow walk out with a cart full of gardening paraphernalia and some "deeply discounted" appliance, hair-care product, or quesadilla maker?), she's expected to help me carry the loot in instead of just merrily skipping in front of me empty handed. Unfortunately, her first assistance attempt was a comical train wreck because when I was looking the other way she dutifully mimicked me and looped one too many plastic bags up her little forearms then toppled over when she attempted to walk toward the house. I'll never forget her darling exasperated expression or the way she protested, "Mama, 'dis is too HAWD!"

This is surely the internal reaction some women have when it comes to Bible study. 'Dis is too hawd! Especially the it's-been-a-while-since-I've-been-in-church or the I've-never-been-in-a-small-group-and-didn't-know-crop-pants-were-required crowd. Because let's admit it—if you've never been in a Bible study before, it does appear to be a bit difficult at first what with all the looking up of verses, filling in blanks, and divulging deep thoughts. So let's make a pact that our study of Mark is going to be a safe place to engage with God, okay? That we're going to be the kind of community where every woman feels comfortable asking questions about Him, sharing the highs and lows of her story, and ultimately leans more fully into the arms of the Jesus we're all aching for.

In light of that goal it's not necessary to choose a single group leader for this study (I can almost hear the audible gasps from the type As reading this!), and may actually be more beneficial to choose a couple of friendly chicks to colead, because that will help make the environment less personality-driven and more participation-driven.

HERE ARE A FEW TIPS TO PROMOTE HEALTHY INVOLVEMENT:

- Establish a no-monopoly chat zone. Encourage everyone to answer at least one question rather than having one big-talker answer all of them.

- Allow for "silence cushions" between questions to give introverts time to formulate their thoughts and participate.

- Throw spitballs at anyone who responds to a question with a basic yes-or-no answer. Okay, maybe spitballs are a tad punitive, but encourage real responses!

- Be quick to listen and slow to give advice or attempt to fix the other chicks' problems in your circle. Just say no to Dr. Phil wannabes!

- Make your best effort to begin and end on time.

- Don't focus on moving through all the material each time you get together; instead, focus on how your small group tribe is moving toward Jesus.

In an effort to make Mark user-friendly, we've created a Bible study book geared toward participation instead of intimidation. We've also segmented it into chunks instead of days, so you can complete the questions when you have time—when your baby's sleeping, when your husband's glued to a football game, or when you're finally home from work and have changed into a pair of comfy sweatpants. The last thing we want is to make the homework so cumbersome and time-consuming that your group dwindles down to non-existent.

Each week starts with a two-page video and group guide. For the first session, you'll just watch the video and get to know each other. Then, during the following week, complete your first week's study. When you gather for the second session, discuss the week one study and watch the second session video.

Your format can depend on your group's size. If your group has few members, discuss the previous week's study first and then watch the video, allowing for some time to discuss the video's questions afterward. If you have a large group, you'll probably want to watch the video first and then combine the discussion of video questions and the previous week's work.

Now, may I encourage you to breathe deeply, smile genuinely (even if it's just to yourself), and turn the page? Then doodle wildly in the margins. Be as honest as possible in every response. And fire away with your thoughts, since few questions have right or wrong answers. Feel free to throw this Bible study book on the floor with gusto if something I've written steps on one of your emotional bruises—or hug it close to your chest when Jesus whispers how valuable you are to Him while you're perusing a passage.

My sincere hope and fervent prayer is that the King of all kings will woo us closer to Himself than ever before this season. That the Holy Spirit—our Comforter and Counselor—will seal in us a profound assurance of God's compassion. And that greater comprehension of His love for us will lead to us becoming more passionate ambassadors of His gospel. I simply Can. Not. Wait. to see how our Savior shows up as we run hard toward Him together! In the meantime, please know that I'm honored and delighted to get to take this divine journey with you.

Warmest regards,

REAL TRUTH

One of the most familiar miracles—this and His resurrection are the only miracles recorded in all four Gospels—is the huge picnic made possible when one little boy's boxed lunch was miraculously multiplied after Jesus blessed it. But interestingly enough, that inspirational story about plenty is preceded by one about poverty. In this segment we'll work our way through Mark 6. We'll see tasks too big but a Lord who always measures up—and makes our little into enough.

> *And he called his twelve disciples together and began sending them out two by two, giving them authority to cast out evil spirits. He told them to take nothing for their journey except a walking stick—no food, no traveler's bag, no money. He allowed them to wear sandals but not to take a change of clothes. "Wherever you go," he said, "stay in the same house until you leave town. But if any place refuses to welcome you or listen to you, shake its dust from your feet as you leave to show that you have abandoned those people to their fate." So the disciples went out, telling everyone they met to repent of their sins and turn to God. And they cast out many demons and healed many sick people, anointing them with olive oil.*
> **MARK 6:7-13, NLT**

What teachings for your life do you see in Mark 6:7-13?

Verse 14 (NLT) says, "Herod Antipas, the king, soon heard about Jesus." Of course we can't be sure what he heard, but it seems that he heard of what the disciples were doing. It says, "because everyone was talking about him," but the context was the disciples' work.

How does the idea that Jesus' fame can be tied to our efforts affect you?

Jesus was becoming known to more and more people, in part because of the work of the disciples. As a result, people began to speculate about Jesus and the source of His power.

What did the people propose as a source of Jesus' miracles according to Mark 6:14-15?

Mark used the idea that Jesus was John the Baptist raised from the dead—now that was some weird speculation—to fill in the back story. Mark relates how Herod reluctantly killed John (vv.16-29). Did you note those words in verse 20, "knowing that he was a good and holy man, he protected him" (NLT)?

Remind me not to depend on someone like Herod to keep me or mine safe. Read on in verses 21-29 to see how Herod cared more about the opinions of others than doing the right thing. Herod had painted himself into a corner, so for Herod to save face, John's head had to go.

So while the Twelve were out there, sojourning all over Galilee without any material provisions for themselves, much less for the crowds of sick and poor people who approached them for help, they received word that John the Baptist, Jesus' first cousin and predecessor, had been murdered. I can only imagine how quickly the air hissed out of their evangelical balloons leaving them hot, sweaty, exhausted, disillusioned, and deflated. Surely most of their get-up-and-go had gotten up and left. They needed to come apart from the hustle and bustle of ministry before they came apart.

How would you rate yourself on the busyness scale?

1	2	3	4	5	6

have to probe for a pulse   *running around cray-cray*
                                                       like your hair's on fire

Are you as drained as I am by all these ups and downs? What did Jesus do when He heard their report in Mark 6:30-32?

Do not miss Jesus making a priority of rest. No wonder the disciples needed a nap. They'd faithfully completed their first mission trip and had complied with the uncomfortable, austere ground rules Jesus established before sending them off regarding not taking any extra food, or tents, or even a change of clothes.

What do you think the disciples learned from the experience of traveling without any extra provisions?

When did you last have to face a situation with less resources than you thought you had to have? How did it go? Did you learn anything from it?

READ PSALM 23. What do you think David meant when he wrote that the Shepherd "makes [us] lie down in green pastures"?

In light of your personal schedule this season, do you find yourself genuinely welcoming more ministry "opportunities" (e.g., baking a casserole for a sick friend or subbing in children's Sunday School even though you've already "done your turn" because they're short a few helpers) or secretly resenting them? Explain your answer.

As is so often true in our modern-day lives, the disciples' respite didn't last nearly long enough because the stillness implied by Mark 6:32 was rudely interrupted by the clamor described in verse 33. Are you surprised that the situation reminds me of a story?

Missy was at a women's conference with me this past weekend. After a day and a half of being asked for hugs and to pose for pictures by dozens of well-meaning event attendees who feel connected to her through social media, she finally reached her limit. While sitting on the potty in the "family" restroom, yet another one of her fans chirped, "Is that Missy I hear in there?" outside the stall. My baby girl's big brown eyes searched mine pleadingly, and then she asked with a loud sigh, "Do I have to hug dat lady too, mama?"

Surely that's what the original twelve were feeling after having their first, much-needed, vacation cut mercilessly short by a bunch of paparazzi types who recognized their getaway boat and ran ahead to the marina to pounce on them the minute they pulled up to the dock. My guess is the band of disciples weren't feeling very hospitable when Jesus stopped and began to talk to the would-be stalkers:

> *Jesus saw the huge crowd as he stepped from the boat, and he had compassion on them because they were like sheep without a shepherd. So he began teaching them many things.*
>
> *Late in the afternoon his disciples came to him and said, "This is a remote place, and it's already getting late. Send the crowds away so they can go to the nearby farms and villages and buy something to eat."*
> **MARK 6:34-36, NLT**

In light of the disciples' state of exhaustion and the burden to deal with a needy crowd, their energy was in short supply. I understand why they encouraged Jesus to shoo the throngs away. These oh-so-human Christ-followers were understandably at the end of their emotional ropes. In addition, they were in the middle of nowhere with a noticeable scarcity of grocery stores and fast-food restaurants.

Have you ever been there? Ever felt like Jesus was asking you for millions when you were having a hard time even scaring up a little spare change?

It reminds me of 1 Kings 17:7-16. Elijah's landlord had a seemingly limited supply of oil, which was a basic necessity for survival in ancient culture. God miraculously replenished the oil Elijah needed.

What basic necessities (i.e., time, money, food, energy) do you need God to replenish for you this season?

I have the tendency to run too long without refueling and run slap out of spiritual and emotional gas. I'm so glad Jesus didn't reprimand the disciples for their exasperated protest about sending the crowds away. Instead He gently pushed them a little further than they were used to going with the question, "What do you have that we can work with?"

But Jesus answered, "You give them something to eat."
They said to him, "We would all have to work a month to earn
enough money to buy that much bread!" Jesus asked them,
"How many loaves of bread do you have? Go and see."
MARK 6:37-38A, NCV

The first medical mission trip I took to Haiti, shortly after I began the adoption process with Missy, was the single most overwhelming one I've ever been on. I've been to a lot of Third World countries over the years and have seen firsthand the heartbreaking effects of poverty, famine, human trafficking, and war. But I never got my hands super dirty for too long. Typically the trip organizer gave my counterparts and me short, preapproved doses of the indigenous people we were hoping to assist. Then they would extricate us from the people's devastating reality and plop us back into a less dangerous environment—like a decent hotel after our brief allotted mission time.

But the Haitian trip had a very different itinerary. Hundreds of rural, impoverished people showed up outside our tin roofed pavilion on the first morning of the project. Many of them had walked all night when they heard the news about a free medical clinic at the base of a mountain. It quickly became an all-hands-on-deck, no-time-for-coddling situation in the sweltering heat. Since I don't have any legitimate medical experience, I was hustled over to the scabies/communicable skin disease/burn wound area.

The expression on my face must've conveyed my complete lack of medical training. The senior nurse who was running our little corner of chaos paused for a few seconds to grab my shoulder, look kindly into my eyes, and say with authoritative encouragement: "We don't have the medicine or supplies necessary to treat life-threatening wounds. We may lose some today, but bathe all of them. Put topical antibiotic on all of their wounds. Hold every baby, and comfort every mama. Just use what you have, and do the best you can."

Just use what you have, and do the best you can.

I think Jesus sent out the Twelve to learn that lesson.

The longer I run hard toward Jesus on this increasingly dark course called earth, the more I realize what sound advice that actually is. We must endeavor to bring the best we have to bear when it comes to loving well those He allows us to rub shoulders with. But we have to trust Him to provide the rest of what people around us need. We can't forget that when Jesus blesses it, even the most meager hors d'oeuvres can feed a multitude:

When they found out, they said, "Five loaves and two fish." Then
Jesus told his followers to have the people sit in groups on the
green grass. So they sat in groups of fifty or a hundred. Jesus
took the five loaves and two fish and, looking up to heaven, he
thanked God for the food. He divided the bread and gave it to
his followers for them to give to the people. Then he divided the
two fish among them all. All the people ate and were satisfied.
The followers filled twelve baskets with the leftover pieces
of bread and fish. There were five thousand men who ate.
MARK 6:38B-44, NCV

The bottom line of this familiar story is: our scarcity + faith in Jesus = more than enough.

Compare 2 Kings 4:1-7 about Elisha (Elijah's successor) and another oil-challenged chick with the widow of Zarephath from 1 Kings 17:8-16. How would you synopsize the spiritual moral of both of their stories?

Mark 6:42 (NCV) says, "All the people ate and were satisfied." How would you define being satisfied, spiritually-speaking? Are you satisfied that way?

WE HOPE YOU ENJOYED THIS SAMPLE FROM *THE GOSPEL OF MARK.*

God's heart is moved by your cries for help, your shouts for joy, your unspoken worries. He may be a God of unparalleled power and authority, but Mark's account of Jesus paints Him as a deeply personal and intimate God too.

In Lisa Harper's 7-session study, you'll follow Jesus through His days of early ministry all the way to the cross, where you'll discover what it means to be the recipient of His excessive compassion and the very reason for His all-consuming passion.

Come discover Jesus like never before.

AVAILABLE WHEREVER BIBLE STUDIES ARE SOLD